MW00608830

IMAGES
of Rail

SAN DIEGO AND ARIZONA RAILWAY
THE IMPOSSIBLE RAILROAD

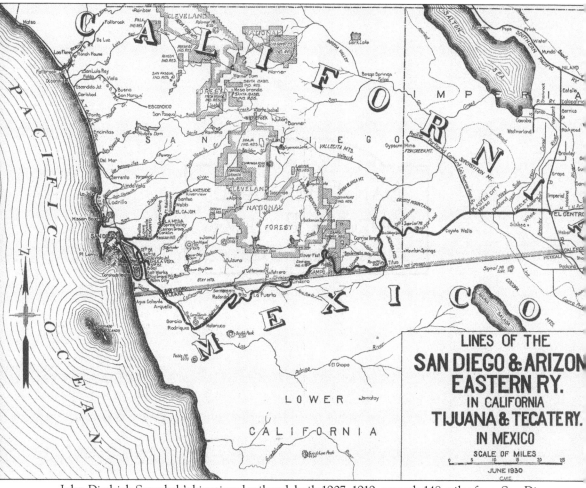

LINES OF THE
SAN DIEGO & ARIZON
EASTERN RY.
IN CALIFORNIA
TIJUANA & TECATE RY.
IN MEXICO
SCALE OF MILES
JUNE 1930
C.M.E.

John Diedrich Spreckels's binational railroad, built 1907–1919, extends 148 miles from San Diego to El Centro, California. Half of the route is curved. Altitude ranges from 3,660 feet in elevation to 49 feet below sea level. The line earned its nickname of "Impossible Railroad" because of the rough terrain on its route. (PSRMA.)

ON THE COVER: San Diego & Arizona Railway locomotive No. 50 is blowing out steam just north of the Mexican border in 1919 while shuttling passengers between San Diego and the racetrack in Tijuana, Mexico. Built in January 1911 by Baldwin, No. 50 is one of only four locomotives bought new by the San Diego & Arizona Railway. (PSRMA-RVD.)

IMAGES
of Rail

SAN DIEGO AND ARIZONA RAILWAY
THE IMPOSSIBLE RAILROAD

Reena Deutsch, Ph.D.

*With the cooperation of the
Pacific Southwest Railway Museum Association*

ARCADIA
PUBLISHING

Copyright © 2011 by Reena Deutsch, Ph.D.
ISBN 9781531653958

Published by Arcadia Publishing
Charleston, South Carolina

Library of Congress Control Number: 2010932483

For all general information, please contact Arcadia Publishing:
Telephone 843-853-2070
Fax 843-853-0044
E-mail sales@arcadiapublishing.com
For customer service and orders:
Toll-Free 1-888-313-2665

Visit us on the Internet at www.arcadiapublishing.com

Dedicated to John Diedrich Spreckels, who continues to inspire folks having an "impossible" dream to persist until it is achieved

The SD&A Railway logo, colored orange, black, and white, was used to promote and advertise the railroad. The emblem contains a steam locomotive riding along the edge of the great abyss known as Carrizo Gorge. During the early life of the railroad, the spelling was "Carriso" but remains "Carrizo" on modern maps. (PSRMA.)

CONTENTS

ACKNOWLEDGMENTS

Many individuals and organizations contributed to the preparation of this book. Most importantly, without cooperation from Pacific Southwest Railway Museum Association (PSRMA) and access to its Southwest Railway Library archives of priceless photographs, the book would not have been possible. Bruce Semelsberger, PSRMA historian, generously shared his time and knowledge, for which I am indebted. Other museum members providing assistance include the PSRMA Board of Directors; Diana Hyatt, president; Ted Kornweibel; Museum Services Department; Lew Wolfgang; Roy Pickering; Jim Lundquist; and Jim Baker. A portion of the author's royalties from sales of this book will go to PSRMA.

I am grateful to Richard Borstadt from International Border Rail Institute and Mountain Empire Historical Society, Vicky DeLong and Mary Oswell at Bonita Historical Society, and John Rotsart, Jim Helt, and John Fiscella of San Diego Model Railroad Museum for their gracious support.

My deep gratitude extends to Michael Reading, Roy Barnes, Kenneth Kahan (former CZRY VP of Operations), Gerald L. Murdock, and Louis S. Adler, Ph.D., PE, who benevolently furnished me with their time, stories, photographs, information, feedback, and other material. I also appreciate René Lamar Scheuerman and George Copenhaver, who shared SD&A(E)-related unpublished manuscripts and photographs.

Feedback about manuscript drafts from Michael Reading, Ann Japenga, Bruce Semelsberger, and John Fiscella was immensely valuable. Thank you. Others to whom I am very thankful are Mark C. DiVecchio (http://www.silogic.com/SDA/SDA.htm) for SD&A postcards, Kenneth Helm and Kit Courter for one-of-a-kind images, and Rick Moore for date estimates based on automobiles in photographs. Also, thank you to SPH&TS's Kerry Sullivan, SD&IV's José Ramos, CZRY's Armando Freire, and MTS.

—Reena Deutsch
San Diego, California
www.ImpossibleRailroad.com

Images in this volume are credited using last names or abbreviations as follows:

Adler	Louis S. Adler, Ph.D., PE	PSRMA Collections	
Barnes	Roy Barnes		
BHS	Bonita Historical Society	PSRMA-BK	Bill Kingston
Courter	Kit Courter	PSRMA-CAV	Clarence Allen Vincent
Deutsch	Reena Deutsch, Ph.D., M.B.A.	PSRMA-ES	Eric Sanders
DiVecchio	Mark C. DiVecchio	PSRMA-FR	Fred Reif
Helm	Kenneth Helm	PSRMA-JS	Jack Stodelle
IBRI	International Border Rail Institute	PSRMA-RVD	Richard V. Dodge
Kahan	Kenneth Kahan		
McGrew	Clarence Alan McGrew		
MEHS	Mountain Empire Historical Society		
Murdock	Gerald L. Murdock		
Reading	Michael Reading		
SDHC	San Diego History Center		
SDMRM	San Diego Model Railroad Museum		
Scheuerman	René Lamar Scheuerman		
PSRMA	San Diego & Arizona Railway Collection, Southwest Railway Library, Pacific Southwest Railway Museum Association		

INTRODUCTION

Throughout its 100+-year history, the San Diego & Arizona (Eastern) Railway developed a chronicle of catastrophes and misfortunes that rival even the most relentless disaster movie. The SD&A(E) suffered floods, landslides, washouts, and a hurricane. Tunnels collapsed and bridges toppled. Labor shortages, financial crises, wars, fires, and disease delayed construction and shut down operations.

If this never-ending struggle occurred in a major city, the disaster-loving public would know all about the so-called "Impossible Railroad." On the contrary, this epic took place in a foreign country and in remote locations. Because the backdrop of much of the turmoil is a beautiful secluded gorge between two backcountry mountain ranges on the edge of the California desert, few will have heard the story until now.

Carrizo Gorge is a blend of contradictions. It is breathtaking and awesome in raw splendor and beauty, yet harsh and barren from arid desert topography. It provided the least gradient for trains to unite their route across a mountain range, but the most difficult terrain through which to construct a railroad. To benefit from the gentle grade meant to penetrate an international boundary.

The unwitting engineer of this combination of calamities and magnificence was a man named Spreckels. Born the son of sugar tycoon Claus Spreckels on August 16, 1853, John Diedrich Spreckels owned many businesses, some of which were destroyed by the Great San Francisco Earthquake of April 18, 1906, and the ensuing fire that burned for four days. The city was in shambles and families were displaced. Rather than rebuild, he packed up his family and moved permanently to southern California's coastal city of San Diego. Its growing population and business opportunities impressed him during previous visits. Over time, he collaborated with his brother Adolph on numerous business ventures. John Spreckels, called "Mr. San Diego," became a millionaire and the wealthiest man in town.

Spreckels recognized that for San Diego to develop commercially, a direct connection eastward to the national rail system was imperative. The existing southern transcontinental railroad stopped short of San Diego by 90 miles, terminating at El Centro in Imperial Valley, California. In June 1906, a secret deal was brokered by the president of Southern Pacific Railroad (SP), Edward Henry Harriman, with several businessmen, including John Spreckels. The others were John's brother Adolph, son John D. Jr., William Clayton, and Harry L. Titus. SP agreed to fund an extension of the line to San Diego. Secrecy shielded Harriman who was unpopular because of considerable monopolistic control over not only SP, but also the Union Pacific, Central Pacific, and other railroads. John Spreckels was admired because of his civic contributions, and he became the public face of the new San Diego & Arizona Railway, incorporated on December 15, 1906.

Based on previous surveys, the best route was selected to avoid the lofty Laguna Mountain range east of San Diego. It went from downtown San Diego, through Mexico for 44 miles (71 kilometers), then back to the United States. The remaining route went from the border to the high point, then sharply descended through rugged Carrizo Gorge to the desert floor, then eastward across the arid agricultural region of Imperial Valley to its terminus in El Centro. The 8-mile Seeley–El Centro route, already built, was leased from SP. Surveyors and engineers dubbed the 148-mile (238-kilometer) rail project the "Impossible Railroad" because of the harsh topography to be conquered. Little did John Spreckels realize how eerily descriptive the nickname would become.

After a ceremonial groundbreaking on September 7, 1907, financial problems began almost immediately and delayed construction until 1909. Fatefully, 1909 was also the year when Harriman died unexpectedly, and so did his flow of money. SP cancelled future payments upon learning of Harriman's clandestine arrangement with Spreckels and sued to recoup $3 million already dispensed. To make up for the funding shortfall, Spreckels reacted by succinctly stating,

"Well then let me do it." And he did, by raising capital, selling assets, and using personal funds skimmed off profits of his other enterprises. Many years later, the lawsuit with SP was settled and dismissed, leaving half ownership split equally between SP and Spreckels.

It took 12 years, two months, one week, and five days to complete the jinxed line, leading to a gold spike ceremony taking place on November 15, 1919. The compelling force behind the successful completion of the SD&A was John Diedrich Spreckels. However, the little "railroad that could" was plagued by adversity. Tunnels caved in, then rebuilt or bypassed altogether; bridges washed away, then restored or filled in. One crisis after another interfered with construction and shut down operations. When in service, commodities were hauled, passengers were transported to eastbound connections, and tourists were attracted to awesome Carrizo Gorge, but the SD&A rarely broke even. Other profitable enterprises provided subsidies.

After Spreckels died in 1926, his heirs struck an agreement for SP to buy their interest in the line, but the sale was not finalized before a series of events inflicted closures and huge expenses on the company. On February 1, 1933, the new "San Diego & Arizona Eastern Railway," now fully owned by SP, was incorporated. During the 1930s, freight revenue profits were lacking and ridership dwindled, leading to heavy losses for SP. Subsequent revenue fluctuated as more challenges and natural disasters attacked the railroad. Keeping the railroad solvent was a constant struggle. Damage from a monster storm in 1976 was the final straw. SP sold the line to an agency formed by the city of San Diego to develop a trolley system.

Since then, a light rail network is in place, freight operators provide service, and a nonprofit museum offers excursions and preservation activities along the railroad's route. The history of the San Diego & Arizona (Eastern) Railway is filled with drama and challenge. It was one man's "impossible" dream. Melville Klauber, president of the San Diego Chamber of Commerce and one of the speakers at the Gold Spike ceremony in 1919, said of Spreckels, "It needed an unusual man, of unusual pluck and unusual patience to put it through." Indeed, Spreckels put it through. Since then, various caretakers, affiliated entities, and interested individuals have kept the dream alive. This book unfolds a chronological pictorial review of the highlights and lowlights of the railroad. The last chapter brings the *Impossible Railroad* story up to the present time. Welcome aboard!

One

CONSTRUCTION
1907–1917
THE IMPOSSIBLE DREAM

John Spreckels, an affluent industrialist from San Francisco, identified profitable opportunities in San Diego when visiting in the late 1800s. After the 1906 San Francisco earthquake and fires, he and his family moved to San Diego. Spreckels, sometimes with silent partner brother Adolph, acquired numerous enterprises: *San Diego Union* and *Tribune* newspapers, water and electric companies, Belmont Park in Mission Beach, First National Bank of San Diego, Spreckels Theatre, all of North Island, Coronado Ferry, Hotel del Coronado, and other hotels. John donated to citizens of nearby Coronado, where he built two homes, the library, and several parks. The Spreckels brothers were major benefactors in San Diego as well.

John owned vast tracts of land, including substantial portions of San Diego communities Mission Beach, Pacific Beach, and Normal Heights. The ambitious entrepreneur developed transportation systems to carry people to his numerous businesses. He purchased failed horse- and cable-drawn trolley routes, consolidated and standardized them, and transformed them to become San Diego Electric Railway. He employed thousands of San Diegans and became well respected. John Spreckels was credited for transforming San Diego, a struggling town, into a major commercial metropolis.

When Spreckels recognized the importance of linking San Diego directly to the eastern rail network, his quest to build a railroad began. Residents supported his effort to remove them from perceived commercial isolation, despite previous failures by others to build a railroad from San Diego. The secrecy of financing arranged with Southern Pacific president E. H. Harriman resulted in the public's reliance on Spreckels to accomplish what others could not. Despite an endless series of challenges and blows, Spreckels's fierce determination to construct the railroad was the driving force behind successful completion of the 148-mile international line.

John Diedrich Spreckels was born in Charleston, South Carolina, on August 16, 1853, the oldest of 11 children. Only three of his siblings survived to adulthood. He worked with his father, sugar tycoon Claus Spreckels, pictured here with John at age 10. In 1877, John Spreckels married Lillie Siebein of Hoboken, New Jersey. They had four children, Grace, Lillie, John D. Jr., and Claus. (IBRI.)

In 1887, Spreckels visited San Diego and made some investments. After relocating to San Diego from San Francisco, John's wealth grew from lucrative business ventures in transportation, communication, utilities, and real estate. Known as the wealthiest man in San Diego, he employed thousands of people and reportedly paid 10 percent of all property taxes in San Diego County. (IBRI.)

Adolph Bernard Spreckels (1857–1924) was president of San Francisco's Golden Gate Park Commission in 1902 and president of Spreckels Sugar Company after his father Claus's death in 1908. He and brother John formed J. D. Spreckels and Brothers. During the turn of the century, John and silent partner Adolph bought failing businesses in San Diego and converted them into profitable enterprises. (PSRMA-FR.)

This image shows downtown San Diego in 1911, five years after Spreckels's relocation. The coastal city, first settled by Spanish missionaries, had a population of approximately 40,000. Spreckels became the public face for San Diego's eastbound railroad. The San Diego & Arizona Railway, initially funded by SP president E. H. Harriman, owes its existence to John D. Spreckels. (PSRMA-ES.)

A groundbreaking ceremony for SD&A took place on the afternoon of September 7, 1907. Spreckels was unable to attend, so Mayor John F. Forward turned the first shovelful. The photograph shows influential land developer and one of San Diego's founding fathers Alonzo Horton, holding his hat. His wife Sarah is seated. The man between them holds the shovel used for the ceremony. (SDHC.)

After groundbreaking, surveys for the SD&A route continued. Land and right-of-ways were acquired throughout the route, and grading contracts were awarded. An economic downturn and financial problems delayed construction, though, until 1909. The building in this image was part of SD&A's facilities near the groundbreaking site. It no longer stands. (IBRI.)

The first new locomotive obtained by the San Diego & Arizona Railway was Class S-23 steam locomotive No. 1, pictured here with employees at the SD&A engine house. It was built in 1909 by Alco in Pittsburgh, configured as 0-6-0, and weighed 107,000 pounds. No. 1 was purchased primarily for construction and scrapped in 1951. (PSRMA.)

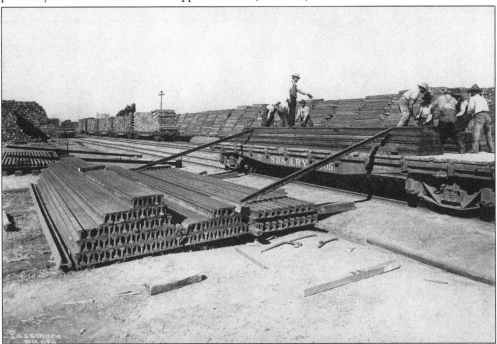

Tons of steel rails and thousands of high-grade redwood ties from Northern California were needed for the 148-mile line. Workers are unloading 75-pound rails in the foreground. Some of the ties are stacked in the background. The first stretch to be built, from San Diego to the Mexican border, is 15½ miles long. (PSRMA.)

Steam shovels, pictured here clearing a cut, dug out the roadbed. Between San Diego and the border, the route climbs fifteen grades, gaining 165 feet of altitude. It drops nearly 70½ feet on 11 descending grades. Only 3 miles of level track are planned. Nearly 1,000 feet of bridges, seven in all, are needed. (PSRMA.)

Tracks reached the border in February 1910. Spreckels negotiated a concession with the Mexican government to build 44 track-miles through Baja California. A separate Mexican corporation, the "Tijuana & Tecate Railway," known as "T&T" (Ferrocarril Tijuana y Tecate), was established. It was owned by SD&A but legally bound to hire mostly Mexican employees, perhaps some of whom are posing here. (PSRMA-CAV.)

As construction continued, SD&A's first excursion occurred on July 29, 1910. The destination was Tijuana Hot Springs, a popular resort 2 miles south of the border. A second train accommodated the overflow turnout of 2,000 people. Passengers proceeded to view Tunnel #1 construction crews at work and, while there, posed for this picture. (SDHC.)

South of Tijuana, two bridges were constructed over the 120-mile-long Tijuana River. The first crossing was 1,050 feet long and completed quickly in 1910. In this undated photograph, a work train is moving over the river at the second crossing, eight miles further upstream. During construction, Tijuana's population was approximately 700. (BHS.)

Widely used since the mid 19th century, steam shovels break up, lift, and move dirt, boulders, and rocks. These two are working in tandem. Four tunnels needed to be dug in Mexico. Two were planned to be 10–11 miles east of Tijuana, and two others will be 6–7 miles east of Tecate. (PSRMA-CAV.)

This Baldwin 2-8-0 Class C-30 saturated steam locomotive, known as No. 50, was photographed just after taking on water. Weighing 137,000 pounds, it was more powerful than No. 1 but reported to have some operational difficulties. Originally built for and purchased by SD&A in January 1911, it pulled work trains during construction and, later, occasional passenger trains. It also handled supply trains and switching. It was scrapped in 1950. (PSRMA-BK.)

Tunnels were numbered #1 through #21, going from west (San Diego terminus) to east (El Centro terminus). Tunnel #1, built in 1910, is shown in the photograph on the right (eastern portal). At 166 feet, 8 inches long, it is lined with 109 feet of concrete and is the shortest tunnel. Tunnel #2, seen in the distance in the photograph below, was located less than a half-mile beyond Tunnel #1. It was much longer at over 300 feet. Both tunnels were bored through fractured, pre-batholithic metavolcanic rock. Fortunately, they maintained their structural integrity despite the fracturing. (PSRMA above, PSRMA-CAV below.)

In 1910, Mexican people were discontented with Pres. Porfirio Diaz's dictatorship and the resulting division of power and wealth. On November 20, an uprising began that interfered with SD&A construction. This image shows revolutionaries crossing the tracks in Tijuana. By May 1911, the entire Mexican railroad workforce had fled, and many non-Mexican workers were recruited during the armed rebellion. (SDHC.)

During the Mexican Revolution, Spreckels claimed to prefer losing everything in Mexico rather than having one man die, but he was pursuaded by work crews to allow them to stay. Trains remained operational, but guarded. Supplies were looted, work crews restrained, and trains fired upon. Witness Mexican rebels boarding the train they hijacked on June 22, 1911. Hours later, hostilities ended when insurgents surrendered while in the caboose. (SDHC.)

This photograph shows the upper Redondo Loop one year after its 1911 construction. The pastoral Redondo Valley provides scenic views from the tracks. To ascend the steep climb while maintaining a reasonable gradient, rails make an almost 180-degree turn and then, after a brief stretch, make another one. (PSRMA.)

In 1914, tracks reached Tecate, Mexico, 7 miles from Lindero at the border. With fewer than 500 inhabitants, Tecate was predominantly an agricultural community. The gang car seen here, propelled by a one-cylinder gasoline engine and followed by a hand-and-leg-powered rail inspection velocipede, shows a T&T section gang heading out to inspect, maintain, or repair tracks near Tecate. (PSRMA-CAV.)

The Tecate depot, built in 1914, is the prominent two-story building in this photograph. The agent who worked there lived upstairs. On September 14, 1914, passenger service from San Diego to Tecate began. Despite absence of development then, Tecate grew to become a thriving industrial and commercial city. (IBRI.)

Many Chinese built the Transcontinental Railroad completed in 1869 and the California Southern in 1881–1885, but most dispersed to settle elsewhere or returned to China afterward. Records documenting Chinese SD&A laborers are unconfirmed. This rare photograph taken in 1914 shows H. Lem Toy, a cook from Canton, China, (right) and helper who provided meals at an SD&A survey camp near the Mexican border. (MEHS.)

In 1914, SD&A purchased two steam locomotives from ALCO in Schenectady. These Class C-31 2-8-0s were dubbed Nos. 101, seen above with train crew on October 7, 1919, and 102 shown below in 1948, both with Vanderbilt tenders. Each nearly doubled the size and power of No. 50. Nos. 1, 50, 101, and 102 comprise the full set of locomotives purchased new by SD&A. Others were acquired used or through borrowing, mergers, and from SP. Initially, engine Nos. 101 and 102 moved construction supplies and mixed trains. After SP leased them during 1917–1919, they were returned to haul heavy freight and were "helpers" for the ascent to Hipass until scrapped in 1953. (IBRI above, PSRMA-BK below.)

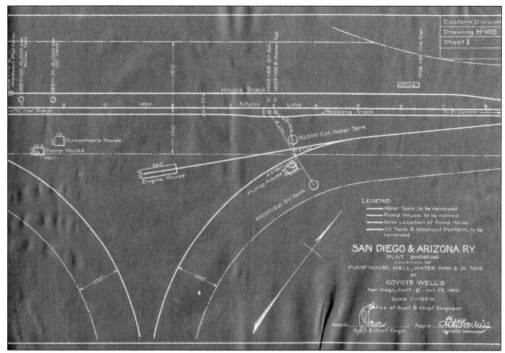

In April 1914, tracks from the east reached Coyote Wells in Imperial Valley, 26 miles west of El Centro. This 1920 engineering drawing of the Coyote Wells site displays the layout. Note three sets of tracks: mainline, passing, and house tracks. Also seen is a wye, an arrangment of tracks used to reverse the direction of a train. (PSRMA.)

The 1,286-foot-long Tunnel #3, shown near completion, was built 6 miles east of Tecate. A half mile further is Tunnel #4, which straddles the international border. It is the only binational railroad tunnel in the United States. Due to stability of the rocks in #4, timber supports were unnecessary except near the more fragile portals. (PSRMA.)

Directly after exiting Tunnel #4, trains cross Campo Creek on a 90-foot-high bridge at Division. This August 1915 image boasts construction progress for the 350-foot-long Lower Campo Creek Viaduct. The Los Angeles factory for the steel supplier, Llewellyn Iron Works, was the scene of a sensational 1910 explosion reportedly due to anti-union activists. (PSRMA-RVD.)

The fifth crossing of Campo Creek is located 17 miles beyond Tunnel #4. The steel bridge, previously referred to as the "high bridge" in the early days but now called Upper Campo Creek Viaduct, is 180 feet tall and 600 feet across. The structure is pictured from the west end during construction. (PSRMA.)

In the winter of 1915–1916, following years of drought, rainmaker Charles Mallory Hatfield (1875–1958) was hired by the city of San Diego to produce rain. Boy, did he! On January 14, 1916, it started to rain. Gently at first, but by the 16th, it became a torrent and continued another two days. Over 12 inches accumulated at Morena Dam, the very spot where Hatfield set up his rainmaking equipment. Some bridges washed out, cattle drowned, wires fell, and roads were blocked. The downpour was unremitting for two more days until finally letting up. Remarkably, damage to SD&A was minimal. Another storm arrived with a vengeance on January 24. It was widespread and intense with ferocious gusts of wind. The Sweetwater Dam was breached with a 90-foot gap on January 30, 1916, shown in this photograph taken that day. Trees and houses were carried away, but little damage to the SD&A mainline occurred from its overspill. (PSRMA-FR.)

The 1916 storm total exceeded 35 inches of rain at Morena Dam. Ironically, Spreckels formerly owned that dam until sold to the city to subsidize construction of his railroad. The ground was saturated. Torrents of runoff from mountains and hills flowed into streams that swelled and spilled over their banks. On January 27, the earth-and-rock-fill 134-foot-high Lower Otay Dam collapsed, releasing 13 billion gallons of water introduced by a wave 40–100 feet high that swept downstream. It took 2½ hours for the reservoir to empty, leaving behind a devastating trail of gravel, mud, rock, and debris. Rain continued to pour onto the waterlogged ground. The SD&A suffered major damage! These two images of destruction at Tijuana River's 1st crossing reflect scenes frequently mirrored along the unfinished line. (PSRMA.)

Flood-damaged 2nd crossing of the Tijuana River shows remaining tower piers. Countless fills washed out, equipment ruined, work camps decimated, and steel trestles flushed. More than one-quarter of SD&A's tracks were washed away! Engine No. 50 derailed, tipped over, and became buried in mud for a month. Up to 20 people died; many were left homeless. (PSRMA.)

Twisted and gnarled bits of the Tijuana River 2nd crossing bridge rear up in a tangled mess downstream in this post-flood photograph. Despite the "Impossible Railroad" reputation, when asked what should happen next, Spreckels was quoted as simply saying "Put it back." In 1928, Rodriguez Dam was constructed nearby for water conservation and flood control. (PSRMA.)

Charles Hatfield, mixing rain-making chemicals in this posed photograph, was never paid. Most accounts attribute this to the city's desire to avoid assuming liability. Reports later surfaced that Hatfield changed his name to Benson and practiced drawing his gun quickly. Hatfield was the inspiration for Burt Lancaster's 1956 film *The Rainmaker*. He died in 1958. (MEHS.)

The caption reads, "First train at Campo, Sept. 16, 1916 over San Diego & Arizona R.R. (Left to right) John F. Forward Sr. who, as mayor of San Diego in 1907 broke ground for the railroad, John D. Spreckels, pioneer builder and financier of the railroad, Alphonso D. Grigsby, old settler at Campo, 'Uncle' Lee Morris, old settler at Campo, Harry L. Titus, Chief Council for Spreckels Companies and San Diego and Arizona R.R. Co." Grigsby presented Spreckels with a bundle of 9-foot-high Sudan grass. (SDHC.)

CAMPO, CALIFORNIA

Fishing—Hunting—Boating

Horseback Riding 50c an hour.

Golf—Tennis—Horse Shoes—Free to Guests

Upon arrival in Campo, Spreckels, Mayor Forward, and traveling companions ate a fried chicken and potatoes lunch in the restaurant at Hotel Campo (shown), hosted by Ed Aiken. A toy locomotive on tin rails with ties made of matches served as table decorations. The visitors did not take advantage of overnight rooms available for $15–20 at this mountain resort located at 3,000 feet in altitude. (PSRMA-CAV.)

The Campo depot, built in 1916 and photographed 60 years later, shows a semaphore that stood idly by as it awaited early trains in need of a signal. The depot was restored to its original condition in 2010. Campo is surrounded by small valleys, oak trees, and picturesque grasslands. (PSRMA.)

On January 1, 1916, train service launched from San Diego to Tijuana's new racetrack. Weeks later, Hatfield's flood wiped it out. After rebuilding and completing the route to Campo, San Diego-to-El Centro service was inaugurated. For 50¢ round-trip, passengers from San Diego disembarked at Campo after a 3½-hour train ride, then boarded a 12-passenger "Auto Chair Car" for El Centro. Horse-drawn conveyances like the one in this undated photograph became obsolete. (PSRMA.)

San Diego and Southeastern Railway's (SD&SE) future was washed out by the 1916 flood. SD&A bought the financially strained shortline the following year. SD&A was already using some SD&SE rolling stock, so the merger was absorbed seamlessly, and extra locomotives and cars supplemented SD&A's scant inventory. Here is SD&SE No. 22, renumbered SD&A No. 11 in 1920. Built in 1881 by Rogers, it was scrapped in 1925. (PSRMA.)

This 1917 photograph taken at Clover Flat, 6 miles east of Campo, shows that unloading 30-foot-long steel rails from a modified flat car took many hands and plenty of teamwork. In that same year, the federal government halted all railroad construction nationwide due to World War I and the need to conserve resources. Single-minded Spreckels would have none of that. He journeyed to Washington, D.C., and convinced authorities and President Wilson of SD&A's importance in the war effort, explaining that if his railroad would be permitted to complete construction, it would provide transportation for troops, equipment, and supplies to San Diego's military installations. His tenacity triumphed and construction resumed. Spreckels's *Impossible Railroad* was the nation's only railroad to receive such permission. Because of the war, though, costs of construction materials soared. Also in 1917, SD&A construction reached Carrizo Gorge. (PSRMA-CAV.)

Two

Carrizo Gorge
1917–1919
Looks Like Heaven, Feels Like Hell

The 11-mile-long Carrizo Gorge, surrounded by arid, desert landscape, is a deep geologic incision carved between the In-Ko-Pah and Jacumba mountain ranges in southeastern San Diego County. Spreckels homesteaded the right-of-way but failed to perform required development soon enough and lost his claim. Consequently, he bought most of both mountain ranges to prevent others from acquiring land rights. Although visually stunning with breathtaking views, rocky hillsides are excruciatingly steep, suggesting the impracticality of building through it. More than 100 curves and a taxing 1.4-percent grade were necessary to maneuver through the rugged terrain.

The Gorge was remote and without facilities in 1917, as it remains today. Workers lived in dreadful conditions to accomplish enormous feats of building 14 trestles and 17 tunnels, often boring through ridiculously hard, unstable granitic rock. Progress was painstakingly slow and, at times, reportedly measured in only inches per day.

Nearby Imperial Valley farm workers were hired for construction but rapidly retreated back to the farms after gaining renewed appreciation for their former living and working conditions. Other laborers came from deep in Mexico, Los Angeles, Northern California, the Pacific Northwest, and anywhere else they could be found. Greeks, Hindus, Swedes, Germans, Norwegians, and Native Americans were among the diverse labor force.

Construction progress was chiefly hindered by lackluster recruitment and low retention of the workforce. Contractors, forced to pay higher wages during war-caused labor shortages, were suspected of intentionally delaying hiring. Extreme summer heat and bitter winter chills were unbearable during the two years of Gorge construction. Water was piped in from nearby springs, but poor hygiene was the standard. Some laborers left because of harsh conditions, others because of their fear of heights. This chapter illustrates utter desolation, merciless living and working conditions, and the majesty of nature's gift of raw beauty experienced by brave and hard-working men building through Carrizo Gorge.

Carrizo Gorge is a deep, awesome valley between two mountain ranges in southern California. Multiple earthquake faults traverse the 11-mile gorge. It was named for the Spanish word *carrizo* that describes reeds growing thick in the seasonally flowing creek at the canyon bottom. SD&A creatively spelled it *Carriso*, but common spelling is Carrizo. This image displays the unforgiving terrain surrounding the creekbed. Among SD&A's 21 tunnels, 17 of them, #5–#21, will be bored through Carrizo Gorge's solid faulted granitic intrusive bedrock that is always hard and often unstable. Two tunnels, #8 and #14, will each stretch almost a half mile between portals. (PSRMA-CAV.)

Before construction, survey teams, like the one preparing instruments in this photograph, tackled intimidating challenges while mapping routes. When in Carrizo Gorge, one surveyor wrote about the 5-mile distance between his worksite and campsite. After bitterly freezing nights, his team dropped layers of clothing while walking to the worksite as it warmed up, retrieving them on the way back as temperatures dropped again. (IBRI.)

When construction in Carrizo Gorge began in 1917, an enormous engineering challenge was to create level grade for the roadbed, since nature provided none. Dynamite and black powder, stacked in metal cans as pictured here, were used for clearing massive mountainous obstacles. Rattlesnakes, 12-hour workdays, and thorny cactus were common. (PSRMA-CAV.)

Dynamite and black powder notwithstanding, digging and blasting through solid rock to build tunnels was backbreaking. Hand tools, picks, and shovels were supplemented by compressed air, steam shovels, and mules. Timber supports were positioned to keep walls and ceilings from caving in. The final cost of building 21 tunnels was $1.8 million. This photograph shows workers laying tracks and ties at the portal of a nearly completed tunnel. (PSRMA-CAV.)

Marsh Brothers and Gardenier's Camp Number 3 is visible in this photograph taken on July 25, 1918. Construction workers were housed and fed here while building Tunnel #6. They were precariously perched on the steep slopes to be near the west end of the tunnel. Imagine the hardships and lack of common amenities while living and building in the Gorge! (PSRMA.)

In Carrizo Gorge, a construction camp was built near each tunnel, except when two tunnels were in close proximity, as shown here. This Utah Construction Company camp included structures both above and below grade. Camps were built anywhere that could be flattened for bunks, tents, and cabins where the men slept and ate. (PSRMA.)

Civilized shelter and provisions were distant. Laborers residing in Huston's camp, shown here at Tunnel #12's west end, just rolled out of bed in the morning to arrive at work. Water was piped in from springs, but showers were forbidden. Barely perceptible are two mules at roadbed level. Many workers in Carrizo Gorge hastily quit after contending with ticks, rats, bees, and prickly plants. (PSRMA.)

our little shack ↓ ↓ air compressor plant

↓ cookhouse

Somebody seems proud of his "little shack" below Tunnel #7, designated by an arrow drawn on margins of the upper photograph. Other arrows point toward the air compressor plant and cookhouse, although it is unclear which structures they are. A tramway down from the roadbed is faintly visible in the foreground. The image to the left presents a bird's-eye view of the same Young and Crook's Camp 1. The slope's gradient was too steep to build closer to the tracks. Hopefully, laborers packed daily lunches, as one trip up in the morning and one trip back down after work was probably sufficiently arduous. Both photographs were taken between 1917 and 1919. (PSRMA.)

On the outskirts of Carrizo Gorge, not far from Jacumba, dirt roads led to the engineering camp pictured here in a July 25, 1918, photograph published by the *San Diego Union*, a newspaper owned by Spreckels. The man wearing a white apron on the left may be the cook. (PSRMA.)

This 1918 image shows the west end of Tunnel #5. One can see completely through the 400-foot-long tunnel. Longer and curvier tunnels may have natural sunlight blocked completely. SD&A's tunnels were carefully engineered to be built from both ends and meet in the middle. No record was found by the author that this strategy ever inadvertently failed. (PSRMA.)

Tunnels were not the only engineering challenges in Carrizo Gorge. Bridges were needed, too. Called "sidehill trestles," they were constructed on wooden "bents" that were cut shorter on the hill side of the roadbed than the canyon side to accommodate severe slopes. Concrete footings anchored both sides to the ground. A curved example is shown here. (Deutsch.)

The topography of Carrizo Gorge required that 14 sidehill trestles be constructed. This 1960s-era image shows five of the "Seven Sisters," a series of seven closely spaced sidehill trestles between Tunnels #18 and #19. They were named after the first seven Sisters of the Order of St. Joseph of Carandelet who walked through the Gorge in 1870 while on a missionary trip between San Diego and Tucson, Arizona. (PSRMA.)

Depicted in this July 1918 photograph taken between Tunnels #8 and #9 are workers dumping rubble and detritus down the mountainside into the chasm of Carrizo Gorge. The material being dumped is referred to as muck. It accumulates when clearing tunnels or leveling roadbeds to flatten the grade for tracks. (PSRMA.)

Gorge laborers take a break for this photo opportunity. From October 1918 through January 1919, almost half of the railroad's workforce became ill with the Spanish flu, a pandemic supervirus that killed millions of people worldwide. 28 SD&A workers died from the deadly influenza. The only other fatality during construction occurred in mid-August 1919 when a cave-in at Tunnel #8 killed a man trapped under the rubble. (PSRMA-CAV.)

On October 6, 1919, one month before construction was completed, this panoramic view of Carrizo Gorge was captured. From this vantage point, tracks are seen zigging and zagging along natural contours of the mountains, winding in and out of tunnels carved through solid rock under elongated, steep ridges of the desert landscape. Trestles linking two high points across ravines are also visible. It is a long way up from the tracks and an even longer way down, sometimes almost 1,000 feet in each direction. In the foreground is the western portal of Tunnel #15, not yet completed. Note the walking path left of the tunnel. Trails were made around every tunnel to facilitate communication and for shuttling wheelbarrows and hand-drawn equipment between both ends of the tunnel. The final cost of building through Carrizo Gorge was $4 million. (PSRMA.)

On Saturday, November 15, 1919, a large crowd of dignitaries, city officials, Mexican delegates, railroad employees, citizens from San Diego and Imperial Valley, reporters, and photographers accompanied John D. Spreckels by rail from San Diego to Carrizo Gorge, where tracks finally met between Tunnels #11 and #12. The train was dubbed "Gold Spike Limited" for the occasion. Standing on a flatcar, Spreckels spoke briefly to the crowd. Afterward, he prepared the "final" spike to connect the SD&A rails (above). He swung. He missed! Spreckels misjudged the angle needed and bent the spike instead. The crowd erupted in laughter as Spreckels took another swing (right). Close inspection of the tracks leads one to hope that this "final" spike was merely ceremonial and not to be taken literally. (PSRMA above, IBRI right.)

It took Spreckels three attempts before successfully driving the spike into its targeted postion. He is shown here trying to straighten it. It also took $18 million, 12 years, 2½ miles of trestles and bridges, and 21 tunnels running 13,385 feet in length if placed end-to-end. Spreckels claimed this defining moment to be the happiest of his life. (McGrew.)

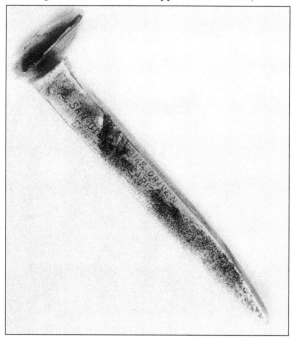

The gold spike ceremony honored completion of a vital transportation link to the nationwide rail system. The genuine gold spike cost $286. On one side was written, "Spike driven, by John D. Spreckels, President." The other side read "Last spike driven, San Diego & Arizona Railway, in Carriso Gorge— November 15, 1919." It was removed shortly after the ceremony to secure it from being stolen. (PSRMA.)

Three

OPERATIONS
PRE-1932
FINALLY ROLLING . . . SOMETIMES

Thousands gathered in San Diego to celebrate what was reported then as the city's most important event ever—the completion of a direct rail connection to the east! Nationwide, newspapers published stories and pictures about this momentous occasion.

Numerous festivities took place during Transcontinental Week, December 1–6, 1919. It launched with the Monday, December 1, arrival of SD&A's first incoming train filled with passengers from El Centro, including Spreckels who commented, "This is the happiest day of my life." That day, declared John D. Spreckels Day, included a parade and elaborate evening banquet at Spreckels's Hotel Del Coronado.

Tuesday was Harbor Day, to celebrate the importance of San Diego's harbor as an outlet for the new railroad. It included an afternoon with water sports and a carnival. Wednesday, Stadium Day, offered athletic events. Thursday's Balboa Park Day brought thousands of merrymakers to enjoy band concerts, community singing, picnics, and organ recitals at the 1,400-acre municipal park, despite a persistent rain.

On Friday and Saturday, December 5 and 6, Spreckels and dignitaries boarded a train for Imperial Valley Days. They made stops along the way where parades welcomed them. John Spreckels addressed the cheering crowds. Imperial Valley residents were as excited and hopeful about the new railroad as San Diegans were on the coast. Rails of steel finally connected the valley with, as San Diego was sometimes called, the "Harbor of the Sun!"

This rare photograph shows people gathered in downtown San Diego on December 1, 1919, greeting the first direct train from the east. Powered by SP locomotives and with Spreckels aboard, the train is just moments away from Union Station. The first freight rail service departed that night with 20 cars. Nine days later, Pullman service to Chicago commenced, switching to Southern Pacific at El Centro. (PSRMA-ES.)

Union Station, depicted in this circa 1920s postcard, was built in 1915 as the Santa Fe Depot by Atchison, Topeka and Santa Fe Railway. It reflects Spanish Colonial Revival Style. A name change occurred when SD&A was completed. San Diego was considered for the western terminus of Santa Fe's transcontinental railroad system, but this distinction ultimately went to Los Angeles. (DiVecchio.)

The official program booklet for Transcontinental Week listed events for December 1–6, 1919, celebrating completion of the SD&A. Everyone was jubilant, delighted about the end of geographic inferiority. The San Diego & Arizona Railway provided a shorter route, by 140 miles, than any other line between Chicago and the Pacific coast. (IBRI.)

Once the line opened, two or three passenger trains ran daily. An overnight Pullman sleeper as part of a mixed train carried both passengers and freight. It took six hours by day and almost nine hours at night to reach El Centro. Some trains continued through to Yuma. This image shows mighty steam locomotive No. 26 and its passenger train sitting at a station. (PSRMA.)

On May 10, 1920, less than six months after train service began, operations unexpectedly screeched to a halt. A landslide crashed down from the steep hills and threatened the west end of Carrizo Gorge's Tunnel #7. Initially, the slide missed the tracks, but two days later, the earth moved again, crushing part of the tunnel and, vividly displayed here, burying sections of track. (PSRMA-CAV.)

Margins of the slide appear obvious from a distance. To clear the roadbed and tunnel, 2,500 25-pound cans of black powder, 100 50-pound boxes of dynamite, 1,000 feet of fuse, and 300 blasting caps were immediately ordered. Dinkey engines, steam shovel drills, batteries, and dump cars were also requisitioned. To place explosives, three shafts 25–35 feet deep and six drill holes 50–60 feet deep were planned. (PSRMA-CAV.)

Workers are carrying kegs of black powder on their shoulders to holes drilled by the drill rig in the distance. A wide range of laborers were needed to get the job done: engineers, cranesmen, firemen, miners, drillers, and oil rig helpers. Waiters and cooks were particularly difficult to recruit and retain. (PSRMA-CAV.)

At 10:15 a.m. on June 4, 1920, none other than Mr. Spreckels himself pulled the switch to detonate explosives engineered to blow up simultaneously. His back is turned to the camera here, just moments before he set off the big bang. A *San Diego Union* article's headline announced "Will blow off mountain's face to stop slides on Arizona Line" to bring attention to the unique situation. (PSRMA.)

The ensuing blast "gave good result but not up to expectations. Looks like between 3 and 4 weeks to again place line in operation," according to a telegraph sent shortly thereafter by Spreckels to Paul Shoup, SP vice president. The detonation, captured above, required 50–60 tons of dynamite and powder. The estimated loss of business and cost of repair was approximately $250,000. (PSRMA-CAV.)

Newsreel photographers from Los Angeles were invited to film the detonation. They lined up along the tracks, awaiting what was later reported to be the largest black powder blast ever. Prior to detonation of explosives, cameramen were required by SD&A to sign a liability release. The railroad insisted on approving descriptions of the event before they were made public. (PSRMA.)

These four steam shovels at work deliver a sense of how much equipment and manpower were needed for the job. After tracks were cleared, 100 feet of the west end of Tunnel #7 had to be rebuilt. The slide itself was almost 600 feet long, 200 feet high, and 200 feet wide. Approximately 120,000 yards of muck were moved. (PSRMA.)

Tunnel #7's closure complicated operational logistics. Passengers were brought by stage or detoured through Los Angeles. To facilitate its shipments, an oil company proposed to pump oil in pipes through or around the tunnel with trains on each end. SD&A denied the request for safety reasons and a desire to speed completion of the line. (PSRMA-CAV.)

The direction of clearing efforts went from west to east. Clearing tracks west of Tunnel #7 and reconstruction of the tunnel's west end proceeded over six weeks. By late June 1920, rails were finally positioned in Tunnel #7, as shown, and the line reopened. Trains were rolling once again. (PSRMA-CAV.)

Daily freight trains carried alfalfa, hay, straw, and construction material such as cement, gravel, clay, and stone. Connections were made in El Centro for destinations farther east or northeast. By the end of 1920, SD&A had under its control 217 freight cars and 36 passenger cars. It did not earn enough to make a profit, though, and expenses exceeded revenue by $250,000. (PSRMA.)

Snow sometimes falls in the higher elevations of the SD&A route. These fellows tossing snowballs circa 1920 are in front of No. 400, SD&A's first caboose, painted cardinal red. The SD&A insignia was approved in 1909 by President Spreckels. He directed that the trademark bearing the SD&A letters with an arrow piercing through them be imprinted on all railcars, stationery, and advertisements. (BHS.)

This annotated image shows one washout among dozens produced by widespread flooding in December 1921. That year's deficit was smaller than in 1920, but upon entering 1922, SD&A's financial position was tenuous at best. Since SP and Spreckels were positioned as both lenders and borrowers for the company, operations were maintained. (PSRMA.)

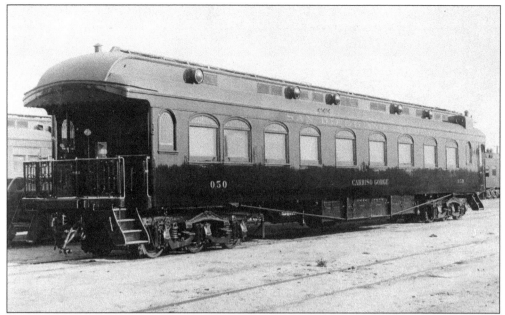

This wooden railcar, built in 1910 by the Pullman Car and Manufacturing Corporation, was purchased in 1922 and custom-converted to a business car for John Spreckels. It included a lounge, office, dining room, two bedrooms, toilet, bathtub, stall shower, galley, pantry, and steward's quarters. Spreckels often entertained in his lavish suite-on-wheels, named "Carriso Gorge" and numbered 050. It weighed over 73 tons and cost $38,952.50. (PSRMA-ES.)

This handsome SD&A crew stands by for another trip on the train. In 1922, the railroad hauled 50,000 carloads of products valued at $50 million. Shipments included 13,000 carloads of canteloupes and melons, 600 carloads of lettuce and vegetables, 85,000 bales of cotton, and 6,000,000 pounds of dairy products, all from Imperial valley. (PSRMA.)

The first SD&A timetable/brochure boasted that passengers "are not bothered with objectionable fumes and smoke . . . , due to the large bore of tunnels, exceptionally light atmosphere and a slight draft continually passing through Carriso Gorge." That arguable statement was excluded in later publications, including this timetable from 1923 that listed 5 stops in Mexico and 13 stops in the United States en route to El Centro. (Reading.)

ALONG THE SAN DIEGO & ARIZONA RAILWAY. IN CARRISO GORGE.

Countering SD&A's earlier assertions, customers created a new meaning for the company's initials: "Slow, Dirty, & Aggravatin'." Brutal seasonal heat and lack of air conditioning required maximum ventilation. Smoke and soot trapped in tunnels entered passenger cars through open windows. Speeds reduced to a crawl while maneuvering around many tight curves. This 1920s postcard shows a train between smoke-choked tunnels. (DiVecchio.)

Carrizo Gorge tunnel lengths ranged between 239 and 2,597 feet. In some of the longer tunnels, riders were thrust into sustained darkness. Other tunnels had either only momentary darkening or constant light shining through the passageways. When out in the open, Carrizo Gorge offered numerous scenic views and thrills for passengers and crews. (PSRMA.)

These sidehill trestles east of Tunnel #6 reflect Carrizo Gorge's extreme pitch. Travelers experienced adventure while viewing some of the oldest rocks in southern California. Millions of years ago, a great sea deposited silt and sand that metamorphosed into hard, dense, fractured rock after intense heating and compression. Depending on time of day and cloud cover, landscape colors vary in tint and hue. (PSRMA-CAV.)

IN CARRISO GORGE. SHOWING TRACK 1000 FEET ABOVE BOTTOM OF GORGE ON SAN DIEGO & ARIZONA RAILWAY

This 1920s-era postcard overlooks Goat Canyon, a tributary of Carrizo Gorge between Tunnels #15 and #16. Trestles are discernible in the distant background on the right. After leaving San Diego, travelers commonly connected with Southern Pacific trains in El Centro that went directly to El Paso, New Orleans, Chicago, Kansas City, New York, New England, and points in between. (DiVecchio.)

As this gentleman applied oil to the main or side rod bearings, he may have been joyous about SD&A's increased revenue from improved freight business and more passengers, or, maybe not. While business was steady and the bottom line moved up, profits were modest at best in the 1920s. (BHS.)

SD&A "helper" stations were located at Hipass (above) and Coyote Wells (below). Helpers were extra locomotives used to nudge trains up the steep climb to Hipass, high point of the line at 3,660 feet above sea level. From Coyote Wells at 272 feet in elevation, Hipass was reached after an uphill 2.2-percent gradient almost to Carrizo Gorge followed by a 1.4-percent gradient through Jacumba, then a 2.2-percent grade thereafter. From Campo to Hipass, the ruling grade was 1.4 percent. The Hipass section foreman's house is seen on the left in the upper image. In the lower image, a 30,000 gallon water tank (left) and 65,000 gallon fuel oil tank (right) are visible. An old wooden passenger car body was used as a station. Buildings no longer stand at either location. (PSRMA-CAV.)

On June 7, 1926, John Spreckels, represented on the right in a bust created in 2005, died at age 72. His legacy lives on. Despite enormous challenges, his "Let me do it" spirit, and his money, kept the *Impossible Railroad* intact. Over his lifetime, Spreckels and brother Adolph presented many gifts to the citizens of San Diego, including an imposing outdoor organ and 2,400-seat pavilion, the only one of its kind, for the 1915–1916 Panama-California Exposition held in San Diego's Balboa Park. The New Year's Eve 1914 dedication was attended by former presidents Teddy Roosevelt and William Taft. Free organ concerts were, and still are, presented regularly from the Spreckels Organ Pavilion, shown below in a photograph taken on May 31, 2010. Upon Spreckels's death, his family members inherited his share of the SD&A and immediately considered looking for a buyer. (Deutsch.)

After its founder's death, the *Impossible Railroad* continued to live up to its reputation. Heavy rainstorms in the desert tend to dump their loads faster than they can be absorbed. That is what occurred in December 1926. A flash flood west of Coyote Wells necessitated heavy equipment, shown here, to shovel sand and replace washed out fill. Clean-up took one month, then operations resumed. (PSRMA-CAV.)

More flooding took place in February 1927, this time along tracks between San Diego and Garcia, Mexico. Additional flooding hit again in 1929. Train service halted until workers repaired damage from immense forces of churning water that washed away fill from beneath rails and bridges. This scene is characteristic post-flood action. (PSRMA-CAV.)

Since construction, Tunnel #15 in Carrizo Gorge showed signs of instability. Historic and geologic records are unclear about the cause: seismic activity, runoff, or a combination. Some faulting on the east end was noted. A culvert, visible on the lower half of this engineering photograph taken after a minor slide, was installed to divert runoff and minimize track damage. (PSRMA.)

Engine No. 1 was seldom used for long hauls. This circa 1920s image shows it pulling a work train, connected to its tender, tank car, and caboose. All SD&A steam engines were powered by oil, not coal. People in the picture are unidentified; Jacumba's Round Mountain looms in the distance. (BHS.)

Steam locomotives were thirsty machines. Heated by oil, water transformed into steam to drive engines that moved locomotives. Water tanks, like the one pictured here, held 10,000–40,000 gallons and were stationed about every 10–25 miles throughout the route. Locomotives took on water through water cranes or spigots, one of which is extended from the right side of this tank. (PSRMA-CAV.)

Historically, velocipedes, Latin for "fast foot," were human-powered. After World War I, railroads used that same term to describe any three-wheeled handcar, including the one-cylinder gasoline-powered Smith Motor Wheel car pictured here circa 1920s and used by SD&A. They were important modes of transportation for track inspectors and probably a welcomed improvement over hand-pumped predecessors. (PSRMA-CAV.)

By 1928, Tijuana Hot Springs, destination of SD&A's first passenger excursion in 1910, was expanded into a fancier resort now called Agua Caliente (Spanish for "hot water"). A generous flow of alcohol during this time of Prohibition and new racetrack in 1929 attracted brisk streams of passengers. En route, travelers crossed the 315-foot-long ballasted deck Otay Creek Bridge, seen in this 1912 photograph. (PSRMA.)

Self-propelled gas-electric motor car No. 42 is on standby to transport passengers to the racetrack in Mexico. It is one of three gas-electric cars, all of which originally belonged to SD&SE. In early years, the border town on the United States side was called Tia Juana (two words). Later the town was renamed San Ysidro. (PSRMA-BK.)

This undated photograph shows the 510-foot-long bridge at Tijuana River's 2nd crossing. It is an open-deck plate girder viaduct. People on the bridge seem to be gazing at the Tijuana River below them. Usually, the river is narrow and tame, or dry. During the 1916 floods, the river washed out parts of this bridge. (PSRMA.)

Looking westward, a passenger train is seen crossing glorious Upper Campo Creek Viaduct, the 180-foot-high, 600-foot-long open-deck girder bridge spanning Stony Canyon west of Campo. Notice the automobile beneath the tall bridge. The dirt road was later paved to became Highway 94. The Campo Indian Reservation surrounds the bridge. (PSRMA.)

Paramount Studio's silent movie *Beggars of Life* was filmed in Carrizo Gorge and released in 1928. To stage a scene depicting a moving train that derails and catches fire, a caboose and flatcar were perched at cliff's edge on tracks mounted for the film, loaded with lumber, then lit on fire. The upper photograph shows the train immediately prior to being set ablaze. The lower photograph presents the inferno in progress, just before it rolls (gets pushed) off the edge in full flame. The wheel sets from the crashed car still remain at the creek bottom below Tunnel #6. Other movies filmed in Carrizo Gorge in the 1920s include *Chasing Choo Choos* starring Monty Banks and *Red Lights* in 1926. (PSRMA-CAV.)

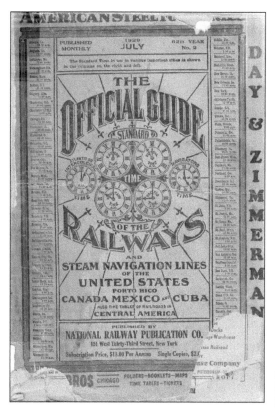

The Official Guide of the Railways provided operating schedules and descriptions for each railroad in service. It was published monthly and widely used. The July 1929 issue, the cover of which is shown here, contains a page with an illustrated SD&A route map stating "On Your California Trip See Carriso Gorge." (SDMRM.)

In 1929, another challenge reared its ugly head for the plagued railroad. Mexico rescinded permission to run trains at night! Freight, responsible for a substantial portion of revenue, only ran at night. Hence, SD&A's bottom line was seriously threatened. This chap in front of the Tijuana depot did not have to wait long for a train, though, since the stoppage was fairly brief. (PSRMA-CAV.)

Four

1932

The Impossible Year

The *Impossible Railroad* consistently operated in the red. Revenue from freight, eastward-connecting passengers, and special excursions was insufficient to achieve prosperity. Repairs and maintenance costs were high, and substantial interest was owed on borrowed funds. Intermittent complaints to the Interstate Commerce Commission and lawsuits resulted in payouts or settlements.

Upon entering into the fateful year of 1932, SD&A owed millions of dollars to creditors and investors. The outlook for its fiscal health, although hopeful, was generally unfavorable. Any hope that existed was short-lived. One costly disaster after another was on the horizon. The only surplus the railroad was destined to have over the next twelve months was a surplus of adversity.

This chapter reviews the unlucky year of 1932. Operations convert to closures, as a wretched string of calamities kept the railroad out of service for almost eight of the 12 months. Still, through a dramatic photographic record, events of misfortune, heartbreaking destruction, and the wrath of nature give way to ensuing scenes of inspirational and creative restoration and renewal of Spreckels's dream.

The photograph on the left was taken of Mexico's Tunnel #3 built in 1915. The year of construction is embedded into the distinguishing stone work adorning the entrance. Its distance end-to-end was in excess of 1,200 feet, and only a pinpoint of light can be seen through it. In the first month of 1932, a fire broke out in the tunnel and burned for four days after the portals were sealed to block inflowing oxygen. Wooden supports collapsed, and so did the center of the roof they supported, resulting in a spacious, but unwanted, skylight. The lower photograph shows some debris that fell onto the tracks that fateful January. (PSRMA.)

This temporary lumber yard was set up east of Tunnel #3. The volume of lumber, including 12-inch-square timbers, reflects the need for significant efforts and resources to repair the tunnel. A steam crane is parked on the tracks to the right. People surrounding the table in front of the shed on the left may be examining tunnel blueprints. (PSRMA.)

On February 11, 1932, this photograph captured the western entrance to Tunnel #3 in the background. In the foreground are contorted rails from inside the tunnel. The fire must have burned at greater than 2,400 degrees Fahrenheit (1,316 degrees Celsius) to melt the steel and cause it to bend and twist into its present shape. (PSRMA.)

The ventilating fan in this February 19, 1932, photograph forced a fresh flow of air into Tunnel #3 while people worked on restoring the tunnel. The primary purposes were to ensure that breathable air was pumped in and to mitigate dust and powdery material likely suspended in the air when ground was disturbed. (PSRMA.)

A muck train, photographed on February 20, 1932, carries rubble removed from Tunnel #3's east end. The damaged roof was never rebuilt. Instead, the tunnel was "daylighted," splitting it into two. A shortened tunnel at 319 feet long remained, still called "Tunnel #3," along with an 897¼-foot-long tunnel newly named "#3½." The cost exceeded $150,000. The railroad was shut down for 45 days while repairs were made. (PSRMA.)

On March 27, 1932, only 17 days after Tunnel #3 was cleared, a bedrock landslide shifted some rocky ground in Carrizo Gorge and caused it to slide down the side of the mountain, threatening to take part of Tunnel #15 with it. Pictured here is a steam crane on a flatcar pouring concrete to buttress the tunnel's eastern opening to prevent collapse. (PSRMA.)

Upon returning the morning after Tunnel #15's portal reinforcement activities, workers found that the mountainside had slid again. This time, the eastern portal was dislodged and separated from the tunnel proper! The damage was deemed irreparable. In this 1970s photograph, folks appear to ponder the damage inside Tunnel #15's east end and wonder where the rest of the tunnel is. (Courter.)

Tunnel #15 was 937 feet long as originally built circa 1918. To replace the condemned tunnel, a much shorter one farther downslope was planned. At 178 feet long, it would be the second shortest tunnel on the line. This photograph captured the April 29, 1932, blast that opened the eastern portal for the new tunnel. (PSRMA-CAV.)

Men are bracing the ceiling at the new tunnel's western end. A wooden platform extends from the slope in this photograph's upper left and provides shelving for lumber storage. It is reached using original Tunnel #15's trail. Nearby, a makeshift chute transfers wood and supplies from above. The gas- or diesel-fueled shovel loads rocks onto the chain-drive Mack truck seen in the foreground. (PSRMA.)

This photograph shows progress made by June 12, 1932. Tunnels were constructed in sections, from the top down. First, 21–22-foot ceilings were built. Muck was passed along wooden planks laid across rafters and dropped down a chute observable on the right. The material then landed in hoppers waiting below on narrow gauge rails. Workers then packed in timbers between the ceiling and walls and the actual rock face to avoid dirt and rocks falling in from the blast hole. This process, called "packing," is demonstrated here. Finally, remaining material blocking the tunnel is cleared out. By June, these workers were probably quite uncomfortable from the desert heat and poor ventilation. However, it is presumed that with more advanced equipment and technical knowledge, the current task proceeded much faster than the original construction's "inches per day" pace. (PSRMA-CAV.)

Track is being positioned from the western side. Ties are lined up and rails are installed farther into the tunnel. In the upper left corner of the picture, one wooden platform is empty, but there is still plenty lumber on the other one. The common name of this brand new tunnel will become "New Tunnel #15." (PSRMA-CAV.)

Notice the positions of the new tunnel, on the right, and the newly abandoned one on the left. The new tunnel was constructed beneath the trail built around the original Tunnel #15. Connecting to the new tunnel looks challenging, since there appears to be an insurmountable void on approach toward the opening. (PSRMA.)

To access the new tunnel, the imposing Goat Canyon will be filled in and bridged. In this scene, cement is mixed onsite for concrete forms for that bridge. Lumber is loaded onto a chute angled downward from track level. The remains of original Tunnel #15's east portal are exposed here in its lopsided stance. (PSRMA.)

The former track alignment served as the staging area for materials and equipment used to build the planned trestle. Lumber was formed into bents, or wooden supports, so tall they were fabricated in multiple sections of the same configuration – but of varying lengths. Some lay on their side just beyond the self-propelled steam crane seen here. New Tunnel #15 construction, occurring simultaneously, is visible on the far right. (PSRMA.)

73

Men are preparing concrete forms for the base of the bridge's west end. The structure was officially designated as Bridge 102.29 or 102A for its distance in miles from San Diego. Some referred to it as the "High Bridge," but it came to be known most commonly as the "Goat Canyon Trestle." (PSRMA)

One-tenth mile east of the original Tunnel #15 is 739-foot-long Tunnel #16. Its western portal is on the extreme right of this image. On the left is a section of the trestle built so far. After completion, a westbound train leaving #16 will immediately transit Goat Canyon on the trestle, then instantly enter New Tunnel #15. (PSRMA.)

Imagine how the crane operator in this June 10, 1932, photograph felt while lowering a bent 185 feet down to the rocky canyon floor. Unobstructed tracks from the east allowed work trains access to the trestle as far as the rails reached. Despite the 2,200-foot altitude, workers were assaulted with relentless desert summer heat, undoubtedly surpassing 100 degrees Fahrenheit. (PSRMA-CAV.)

As all others in Carrizo Gorge, this trestle was built out of wood, not steel, due to periodic extreme daily temperature variations of more than 75 degrees Fahrenheit. Excessive heating and cooling promotes metal expansion and contraction, causing it to become fatigued and unstable. When complete, the Goat Canyon Trestle will contain 157,000 linear feet of lumber! Superb views of Carrizo Gorge will be a bonus. (PSRMA.)

75

This structure, called the "mud shed" by the photographer, served as a makeshift lunchroom. It is inside the concrete extension of original Tunnel #15, built to stabilize the tunnel before abandonment (See page 69). After slaving away in the hot July sun at daunting heights and breathing in construction-generated particulates, these workers must have welcomed downtime in the shade. (PSRMA-CAV.)

This bird's-eye view of essentially completed Goat Canyon Trestle accentuates the 15-degree curvature smoothly spanning the canyon between New Tunnel #15 (unseen on left) and #16 (on right). Notice the footpath around Tunnel #16. Reaching the trestle other than by rail, hard-core hiking, or helicopter is nearly impossible. Altogether, the new rail alignment stretched 0.44 miles. (PSRMA-BK.)

The railroad finally reopened on July 6, 1932, 101 days post-landslide! This contemporary view of magnificent 633-foot-long, 185-foot-high Goat Canyon Trestle reveals the elaborate lattice of intricate web-like arrangements of bents, piles, and timber, perhaps reminiscent of a childhood collection of Tinkertoys. People are barely discernible on the deck. SD&A was rolling again, but hardships did not end. Erosion-pushed boulders periodically roll down and hit bridge footings, even today. (Deutsch.)

On October 22, 1932, barely three months following the line's reopening, another disaster hit the chronically cursed railroad. Fire in Tunnel #7 caused severe damage. Due to instability of the hillside, engineers decided to modify the route and detour around the doomed tunnel. The bypass required seven harrowing 20-degree curves. This photograph shows the abandoned tunnel's eastern opening and part of its bypass. (Scheuerman.)

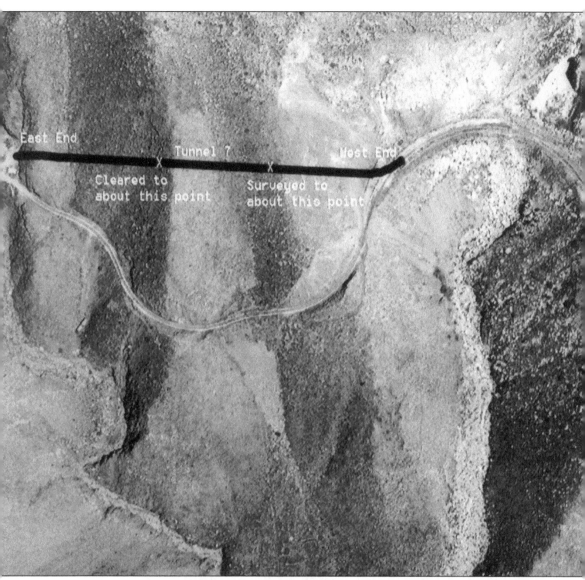

In 1920, when a landslide caused the first closure of Tunnel #7 shortly after SD&A service began, the *San Diego Union* stated, "This is the only place in the gorge that has given trouble of any consequence since the line was placed in operation on December 1 of last year." Unbeknownst to the railroad, that "place in the gorge" was the forerunner of much more trouble. Almost 13 years later, bends and turns constructed to sidestep abandoned Tunnel #7 slowed trains down to a sluggish crawl. This modern-day annotated image presents an aerial view of the position of the (coincidentally) 1932-foot-long tunnel (thickened line) and the wiggly curvature of its bypass. The blaze causing abandonment of Tunnel #7 was the third of three major catastrophes bombarding the railroad in 1932 and put into question whether the SD&A could survive. The *Impossible Railroad* remained out of service into January 1933. (Reading.)

Five

OPERATIONS
POST-1932
LET'S KEEP IT ROLLING

According to one dictionary, a phoenix is "a bird in Egyptian mythology that lived in the desert for 500 years and then consumed itself by fire, later to rise renewed from its ashes." The SD&A was not around that long, yet it displays some striking similarities to the mythical phoenix. During 1932, two tunnels were destroyed by fire, and another by landslide. Two of those, plus part of the third, were unsalvageable and permanently dropped from the route. After being incinerated by fire and more, the railroad appeared to have risen from its own ashes.

An exciting consequence of the disastrous events of 1932 was engineering and construction of the remarkable Goat Canyon Trestle. Claims about it include: "tallest curved trestle in the world," "biggest wooden trestle in North America," "largest curved wooden trestle," etc. No reliable documentation to date has been found to support any of these assertions. Nonetheless, it is a popular symbol of the line, and its very remoteness seems to add to the mystique.

SD&A's unplanned infrastructure rehabilitation delivered a tremendous financial blow to the company's viability, especially in light of its historically meager revenue. Outsiders wondered why its owners continued to operate.

When John D. Spreckels was alive, he followed his dream, apparently his obsession, to do whatever it took to make the line succeed. His heirs, on the other hand, were not so passionate when they inherited a half-interest in his money pit. They wanted to rid themselves of the financial drain. It would be sensible that Southern Pacific, the other half-interest owner, would want to give up the *Impossible Railroad*, too. Nevertheless, SP continued to dispense funds to sustain it. Some say that SP intended to prevent its major competitor, the Santa Fe Railroad, from acquiring long-haul freight business from and to San Diego currently carried along SD&A's connection to SP's system. This chapter describes operations and important changes over the next several decades, even as misfortunes persist.

After Spreckels's heirs received John D.'s railroad, they struggled to keep it alive, despite never-ending turmoil and financial challenges. Unsurprisingly, they wanted to unload the burden and were eventually successful at negotiating a sale with Southern Pacific. On February 24, 1932, permission was requested from the Interstate Commerce Commission for change of ownership. On October 24, 1932, two days after the Tunnel #7 fire, permission was granted. On February 1, 1933, transfer to SP was finalized and the San Diego & Arizona Railway, the "Impossible Railroad," no longer existed! The "San Diego & Arizona Eastern Railway" came into being on that day, wholly owned and operated by Southern Pacific. The sales price was $2.8 million. Interestingly, since SP was half-owner of the SD&A, it paid itself $1.8M for its $17.4M investment. The Spreckels clan received only $1M for the $11.4M it paid. Does the unprofitable essence of the *Impossible Railroad* linger? (PSRMA.)

Engine No. 12, re-lettered to reflect new ownership, poses at the San Diego engine house in the 1930s. Closures in 1932 reduced the railroad's workforce to fewer than 300 employees and freight to only 6,525 carloads. That year's operating deficit increased to over $600,000, compared to $51,000 in 1931. Throughout the 1930s, freight service remained steady, but moderate losses persisted. (PSRMA.)

Ridership declined significantly during the 1930s, although magnificent Carrizo Gorge still attracted travelers. Steep cuts, winding curves, and forever vistas were awe-inspiring. The deficit shrank dramatically to $81,000 the first year under SP's full ownership. This was largely because debts, including interest owed to creditors, were eliminated by SD&A's sale. (PSRMA.)

The serpentine transit through Carrizo Gorge is apparent from this photograph of a train meandering along one of the *Seven Sisters* between Tunnels #18 and #19. Top speed allowed in the Gorge was 15 miles per hour to prevent derailment on the undulating curves while passing through the ancient, rocky canyon. (PSRMA-FR.)

Tunnel #7 and #8 trails are visible in the background of this marvelous photograph taken from above Tunnel #6. Wheel sets from the 1928 *Beggars of Life* crash rest on the hillside and in the creekbed below the train. After sufficient rain, barren hillsides green up and explode into bouquets of color provided by opportunistic desert wildflowers. (IBRI.)

Frequent runs from San Diego to Tijuana and Agua Caliente, in Mexico, attracted steady streams of ticket-buying passengers through the early 1930s. The route maintained high demand after acquisition by SP. Free-flowing alcohol during Prohibition and Agua Caliente's horse racetrack were the main draws. Later in 1933, Prohibition was repealed and California legalized parimutuel gambling. People no longer needed to travel below the border to satisfy their thirst and gambling urges. Passenger revenue plummeted. GE gas-electric cars, like that shown above in February 1933, were used for those popular trips but discontinued around 1934. The lower photograph shows the back of the racetrack grandstand in 1916. (PSRMA.)

This is the last steam locomotive that SD&AE purchased. It is No. 3, resting at the San Diego yards in this 1930s photograph. The 0-6-0 Class S-5 Baldwin, weighing 145,140 pounds, was built in 1902. SD&AE bought it in July 1936 from SP, and sold it four years later. (PSRMA-BK.)

This locomotive is parked at Union Station. A full baggage cart waits alongside the train. Widespread increases in automobile ownership and more, longer, and improved roads impacted revenue. SD&AE operations were largely subsidized by more profitable activities under SP's ownership, somewhat reminiscent of the "Let me do it" spirit of John D. Spreckels. (PSRMA-BK.)

Promotion and advertising to drum up business took many forms. In 1938, the SD&AE Employees' Business-Getting Committee was organized to encourage staff to "be on the lookout for prospective rail business." Time and location of this billboard is unknown, as is whether or not the committee was responsible for it. (PSRMA.)

On October 15, 1939, the Los Angeles Railway Boosters Club chartered a trip to Carrizo Gorge. This photograph captures passengers experiencing the vast openness of that gigantic rift surrounded by hard rock and desert terrain. The nine-car train waits at Carrizo Gorge siding. Tunnel #11 is in the background. (PSRMA.)

During the 1939 railfan excursion, participants climbed atop locomotive helper No. 102's tender while stopped (hopefully) on a trestle. Probably mothers or wives of these daring gentlemen did not get to weigh in on their decision. Behind the locomotive, or rather, ahead of the locomotive pushing from behind, is a passenger observation car. (PSRMA.)

Ridership dropped throughout the mid- to late-1930s, despite special passenger excursions and charters for railfans, photographers, and the general public. Like the passengers about to enter dark Tunnel #19 pictured here, SD&AE must have wondered if there would be any light at the end of their tunnel of losses. (PSRMA.)

The dramatic Goat Canyon Trestle is remote and vulnerable to fires from lightning and vandals. The arid desert climate leaves everything bone-dry. Temperatures often rise above 100 degrees Fahrenheit (38 degrees Celsius). A resident watchman was on duty round-the-clock, and block signals warned in case of fire or obstructions. To defend against a catastrophic inferno, a sophisticated firefighting sytem was installed. Note the black tank upslope in the upper photograph, dated 1939, and pipe leading down from it. The tank holds 12,500 gallons of water that flow down to a collection of valves, pipes, hoses, nozzles, and outlets that direct water to different levels of the bridge. The elaborate, manually operated system is detailed in the diagram below. (PSRMA.)

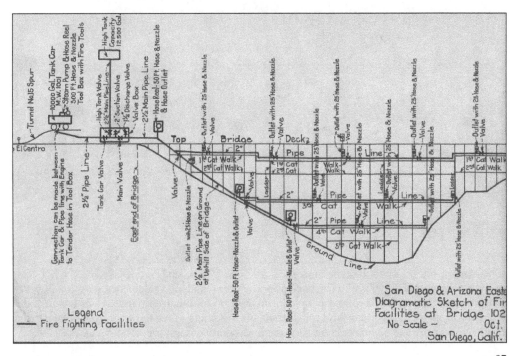

The Goat Canyon Trestle is barely visible from the photographer's perspective looking southward (railroad west) through Carrizo Gorge. During the 1930s, a vocal segment of the population pressured the railroad into preserving this sprawling desert expanse. Some called for a National Park. Despite concerns about structures along the tracks, SP/SD&AE donated nearly all of Carrizo Gorge for public parkland. Most of the land eventually transferred to Anza-Borrego Desert State Park. Some people assumed it was a tax-saving donation, but annual property taxes were less than $50. It has also been suggested that politics played a role in the donation. (PSRMA.)

One of many setouts for motorcars (motorized railcars, or "speeders") is displayed on the right side of the tracks, with Tunnel #16 in the background. After replacing velocipedes, gasoline-powered motorcars transported two to four people for inspection and maintainance. Prior to scheduled trains, workers rotated the cars and rolled them off to setouts so regular trains could safely pass. Most setouts were less elaborate than this one in decorative flagstone. (PSRMA-CAV.)

After World War II broke out in 1941, revenue traffic swelled to peak levels. SD&AE offered discounted tickets to recruits who packed trains headed for San Diego, often accompanied by their families. There was heavy demand for supplies and equipment from manufacturing plants and military bases in or close to San Diego. (PSRMA.)

During the war, freight trains, like this one carrying an unidentified ride-along, hauled 20,554 carloads of commodities such as hay, alfalfa, citrus, salt, lumber, and cement. In 1943, SD&AE transported 1½ million car-miles of freight. Passenger service income surpassed a healthy $436,000. Unfortunately, the record $2,000,000 in revenue was offset by expenses, resulting in a disappointing $11,000 operating deficit. (PSRMA.)

In 1944, SD&AE moved the most freight ever, 27,045 carloads! Over 20 percent originated from North Island Naval Air Station. 1,600 carloads carried products from Cerveceria de Tecate (Tecate Brewery), with volume more than doubling in 1945. Engine No. 102 is shown in this undated photograph alongside San Diego's electric generating plant, built and formerly owned by Spreckels. (PSRMA-CAV.)

Despite elevated revenue and a full contingent of steam at the 1917-built seven-stall engine house, SD&AE's postwar financial condition was bleak. The net operating deficit in 1945 approached $90,000. Ironically, railroads nationwide commonly transported cement, used to build ever-growing highway systems with far-reaching tentacles that ultimately choked life out of railway systems. (PSRMA-BK.)

These cars photographed at SD&AE's San Diego freight house on January 10, 1948, reflect automobile styles of that era. Cars also represent why increasing numbers of travelers no longer needed trains to get to their destinations. Passenger-carrying business suffered and was headed toward unsustainable levels. A valuable collection of SD&A(E) documents and artifacts was rescued from a dumpster here before the building was demolished circa 1980. (PSRMA.)

SP locomotive No. 2370 is operating as SD&AE train No. 363. Passengers and crew passed routine customs inspections when returning from Mexico on June 15, 1948, when this photograph was taken of the border-crossing at Tijuana. When crossing into the United States from Tecate, customs inspection takes place in Campo, six miles north of the border. (PSRMA.)

Despite the railroad's dismal financial outlook, a joyous occasion happened on July 1, 1949. These proud employees of SD&AE's San Diego Office accepted the Gold Pan Award for highest percentage of passenger sales during the month of May. The ceremony was held at the San Diego Club. Traffic Manager Thomas Fielding holds the award. (Adler.)

While passenger business was waning in the late 1940s, the SD&AE had a special trip for railroad employees and their families and friends on October 16, 1949. Passengers in the photograph to the right look like they are returning to the train after having an opportunity to leave it and wander around Carrizo Gorge. The little six-year-old boy in the foreground, Lou Adler, appears to be headed in the wrong direction. His father, Mannie L. Adler, was the SD&AE Traveling Freight and Passenger Agent. The lower image shows one of the excursion's guests getting a close-up look at the Goat Canyon Trestle. (Adler.)

In the 1950s, business plummeted considerably. The line could not compete against improved highways and automobiles providing door-to-door service at the traveler's convenience. This collision between an SD&AE steam locomotive and a bus probably was not responsible for the dropoff, but it appears to portend the destiny for the ill-fated railroad. (PSRMA.)

This scene reveals a gloomy, dreary, rainy Thursday in San Diego. Puddles along Union Depot tracks greeted travelers as layers of sadness permeated the air. On January 11, 1951, passengers boarded this SD&AE train in San Diego for the very last time. Somebody remarked that even the skies shed tears. In the cab of SP steam locomotive No. 2373 on Union Station's Track 3, Fireman E. J. Rankin commented to Engineer Chris Brown on the last day of passenger service, "Pretty lousy day for the last run." The No. 362 train, shown here, departed 15 minutes late at 7:20 AM but arrived on time in El Centro at 12:20 PM under clear skies and sunshine. Permission to abandon passenger service was granted by the ICC after SD&AE's annual passenger operational losses were reported to exceed $430,000. (PSRMA-JS.)

When the first train left Union Depot in 1919, San Diego's population was only 74,000. The city grew to a population of over 330,000 by the time of the last train in 1951. Direct passenger service between San Diego and El Centro terminated after this final run. This was truly the end of a grand era for San Diego. (PSRMA.)

A. E. Keller was the conductor when these folks pictured in this dimly lit railcar were among the fortunate 169 travelers to experience the historic last ride ending a 31-year run. Previously, through-trains traveled nearly empty. Passenger service within Mexico, as a mixed train, continued until 1963 due to contract obligations with the Mexican government but was no longer available north of the border. (PSRMA-ES.)

SD&AE employee Roy Barnes's camera framed the moment after the historic last train exited from Tunnel #21, the final tunnel en route from San Diego to El Centro. After January 11, 1951, the mighty SD&AE was exclusively a freight hauler in the United States. This service continued uninterrupted; that is, uninterrupted until the *Impossible Railroad* curse emerged again. (Barnes.)

What, again? Yes, the *Impossible Railroad* met another obstacle soon after curtailing passenger service. In July 1951, flash floods roared through parts of Carrizo Gorge and halted operations. Rocks buried rails for over 200 feet between Tunnels #9 and #10. This scene shows the east portal of Tunnel #9. At least three other tunnels were blocked, too. Service resumed shortly after repairs were made. (PSRMA-CAV.)

The railroad switched from steam to diesel in the early 1950s. This 1951 action scene shows SD&AE's first diesel-electric locomotive (Baldwin AS616, 160 tons) as it transits between Tunnels #20 and #21 west of Dos Cabezas. All SD&AE diesels were transferred from SP's inventory; none were purchased. For added efficiency, multiple locomotives were sometimes connected for extra power but under one engineer's control. (Barnes.)

Dos Cabezas section crew quarters, surrounded by wind-tilted tamarisk trees, are seen here circa 1950. The foreman's house, a 1940s-built concrete telephone booth, and a ramp for loading limestone into hopper cars are also at Dos Cabezas. The buildings have since been demolished by vandals, but remnants of foundations and the loading dock still remain. Evidence of early Kumeyaay Indian presence is nearby. (Barnes.)

This 30,000-gallon metal water tank at Dos Cabezas, next to a tool shed, was supplied with water piped two miles from a spring. In 1946, it replaced the original 40,000-gallon redwood tank. Today, the tank still stands on the original base. At 1,720 feet in elevation, Dos Cabezas (Spanish for "two heads") was named after two nearby natural rock formations, each of which resembles a head. (Barnes.)

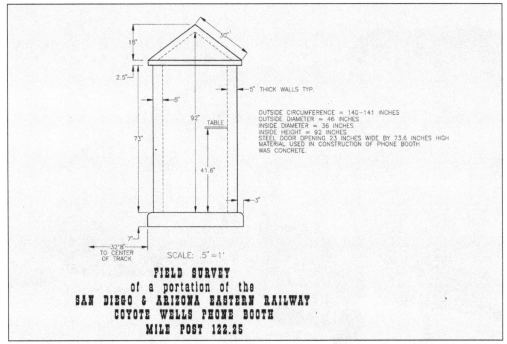

18"   30"

2.5"

5"   5" THICK WALLS TYP.

92"   TABLE

OUTSIDE CIRCUMFERENCE = 140-141 INCHES
OUTSIDE DIAMETER = 46 INCHES
INSIDE DIAMETER = 36 INCHES
INSIDE HEIGHT = 92 INCHES
STEEL DOOR OPENING 23 INCHES WIDE BY 73.6 INCHES HIGH
MATERIAL USED IN CONSTRUCTION OF PHONE BOOTH
WAS CONCRETE.

73"

41.6"

3"

7"

32'8"
TO CENTER
OF TRACK   SCALE: .5" = 1'

FIELD SURVEY
of a portation of the
SAN DIEGO & ARIZONA EASTERN RAILWAY
COYOTE WELLS PHONE BOOTH
MILE POST 122.25

A few steam engines were retained as helpers to supplement diesels. While Hipass station was maintained for helpers at the high point of the line, Coyote Wells helper station supported them from the lowlands in Imperial Valley. This drawing illustrates dimensions of a concrete telephone booth at Coyote Wells. It was identical to others placed throughout the line in the 1940s. (PSRMA.)

Downsizing after passenger service ended meant closing stations and abandoning buildings. One depot used until 1951, then closed, was the one in Jacumba, shown here some years later. It remained functioning as a freight station. A rusty tank car sits beside the tracks in the middle of the picture and the depot building itself is to the right of it. (SDMRM.)

Leora and Roy Barnes smile while having a spot of tea at an old SD&A construction campsite below Tunnel #7. The company had reason to smile, too. Profit finally materialized post-1950, assisted by positive cash flow from the Korean War, cutting passenger service, and changing to diesels. Not much profit, but absence of deficit was considered a good thing for the hapless railroad. (Barnes.)

In the summer of 1956, leafhoppers invaded vegetation along 13 miles of SD&AE's right-of-way in Imperial Valley. The sap-sucking insects not only harmed the flora because of their feeding habits but also transmitted pathogens to the plants. The railroad arranged for aerial pesticide treatment between Dixieland and El Centro. (PSRMA.)

On May 5, 1965, a student engineer throttled up too soon on Tunnel #7's bypass curves his first day of work. Two trailers loaded with Coors beer on a derailed flatcar, shown, and one yellow boxcar were damaged, so over the cliff they went. The boxcar, flatcar, and one trailer are still visible from the roadbed. The other trailer rests at the bottom of the Gorge. (Reading.)

Starting as an 18-year-old SP messenger boy in 1920, Mannie Adler retired as SD&AE's Freight and Passenger Agent in 1967. Rail passes for himself and his wife, shown here, are both valid for unlimited travel 1966–1970 on SP routes. While on the job, Adler rode trains with the San Diego State University football team to their away games and played poker with team coaches. (Adler.)

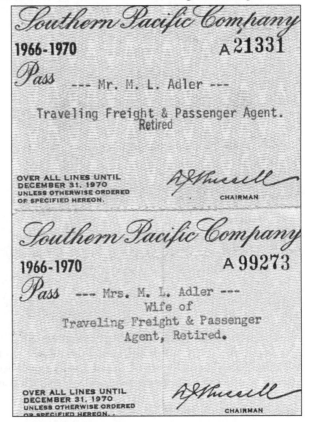

After 1951 and through the 1960s, freight business progressed uneventfully. For this period, records of substantial flash floods, landslides, pandemics, and other bothersome challenges were not encountered. This image reflects a train slithering through the Gorge in the 1960s while exiting Tunnel #10 and heading towards Carrizo Gorge siding on the other side of Tunnel #11. (PSRMA.)

Lined up in this July 1968 photograph in downtown San Diego's freight yard are SP Nos. 5106, 5119, and 5101. These 70-ton GE switchers were intended to move railcars around. Switchers assemble cars for an outbound train and disassemble incoming trains. Rarely do switchers move trains over long distances. Within two years, SD&AE would not own a single locomotive. All would be leased. (SDMRM.)

On May 20, 1970, ownership of Tijuana & Tecate Railway Company was transferred to one of Mexico's national railways. SP received $300,000 and was free to operate anytime, paying the Mexican company $12 per loaded railcar, $4.80 if empty. Due to language barriers, SD&AE was likely the only American railroad where stationmasters still communicated by telegraph. This view is framed by the arch from Mexico's Tunnel #2. (PSRMA.)

This freight train is leaving Tunnel #4 and crossing over Lower Campo Creek Viaduct. SD&AE's typical eastbound cargo included canned tuna, salt, tomatoes, celery, and cabbage. Beer, building materials, grains, and various supplies were often hauled westward. Business ran smoothly with modest revenue through the early 1970s. Then, income declined. A deficit reared its ugly head again. The *Impossible Railroad* was accumulating substantial debt. (PSRMA.)

The last thing the struggling railroad needed was another disaster, yet another one struck. On September 10, 1976, a tropical storm that formed in the eastern Pacific Ocean moved up the Sea of Cortez east of Baja California, Mexico. Wind speeds reached 80 miles per hour. Technically, it was a hurricane for only six hours, then it weakened to a tropical depression at the U.S.-Mexico border. Nonetheless, it has been known as "Hurricane" Kathleen ever since. The storm moved inland rapidly, causing catastrophic destruction. Over one-half of the Imperial Valley desert town of Ocotillo through which the SD&AE passed was buried or washed away. Sand, rocks, and debris were carried afar, then dropped in place. These are remnants of tracks in the wake of the storm in that part of the desert. (Barnes.)

Kathleen cut her wide swathe of destruction throughout southeastern California as this photograph so vividly illustrates. Rainfall exceeded 10 inches in the nearby Laguna Mountains and probably close to that in the desert. Widespread damage and flooding also hit Mexico, Arizona, and New Mexico. In total, the storm caused over $160 million damage and, by some reports, left at least six people dead. (Barnes.)

This powerful image demonstrates destruction outside Tunnel #8's western portal. Throughout SD&AE's "Desert Line" – the stretch between Division and Plaster City – some tracks and fills were swept away and other tracks were buried or dangling over nothingness. Eight trestles were damaged, with three of them completely annihilated. The unsupported telephone line hints at Kathleen's ruthless impact on communications. (PSRMA-ES.)

When torrents of water extruded their ferocity, massive boulders slid down the mountainside, building up speed and power while tumbling hundreds of feet. Behold tracks at Tunnel #12's west end. They lost the competition against the bouncing boulders. An eyewitness claimed that the Goat Canyon Trestle deck and tracks settled a few inches and sagged, and 75 feet of trestle were left unsupported! (PSRMA-ES.)

Two years after Kathleen, backpackers explored the damage. Here they stand at the edge of an abyss west of Tunnel #12. Compare it to the slight void under droopy tracks in the previous photograph. Unchecked erosion left its mark. Storm damage impacted 89 locations over the Desert Line's 70 track-miles. Notorious Kathleen will live on in infamy as a key part of the *Impossible Railroad* story. (Courter.)

Rocks in the Gorge may be the oldest in Southern California, but they were no match for the potent force of Kathleen's intense downpour and runoff. After Kathleen, a speeder near Tunnel #8 was blocked by boulders washed down from above. Jacumba railroad employees abandoned it after another rockfall buried the tracks in the other direction. Target practice anyone? (PSRMA-ES.)

Gerald Murdock photographed Ocotillo's demolition, as shown, and made repair estimates of Kathleen's devastation while on an SP storm evaluation team. Murdock reported that five bents of the Goat Canyon Trestle hung in mid-air after their footings were destroyed. Later, as engineer of maintenance, he returned to work on reconstruction of the roadbed and repair to the landmark trestle. Of tunnels receiving no serious damage, he stated "It was the finest tunnel work I've ever seen." (Murdock.)

Murdock's inspection route extended to Jacumba, 4 miles west of Carrizo Gorge's first tunnel. Not much damage was found in the quiet little town known mostly for mining, soothing hot springs, and the railroad. At the Jacumba station was a tank trailer and rail-modified fire engine built from a 1931 Ford Model AA truck, shown in the upper photograph. The truck was acquired in 1933 to protect fire-prone wooden trestles in the Gorge, including the newly constructed Goat Canyon Trestle. In 1980, it was transported to the California State Railroad Museum where it was restored in 1994 and is still operable. The ensuing masterpiece is displayed in the lower image. (Murdock above, PSRMA below.)

Witness the considerable damage at Titus near Jacumba. Major chunks of Interstate 8, in the background, were removed by the powerful flooding. Damage imposed on the tracks, trestles, and fill was so extensive that SP petitioned the ICC for abandonment in 1977. It claimed repairs, estimated at $1,270,000, were unjustified because the previous year's loss was over $1 million. The ICC denied SP's request in 1978. (PSRMA-ES.)

Discussions between SP and a new transit agency of the city of San Diego led to SD&AE's sale, provided that SP fully restore the railroad to operating condition, including these tracks west of Tunnel #15. Gasp! Not what SP wanted, but at last it could unload its unprofitable encumbrance. The sale included a branch line to El Cajon but excluded the Mexican and Plaster City-El Centro segments. (Barnes.)

U.S. Gypsum Company (USG) provided steady and profitable freight business between Plaster City and El Centro, making it worthwhile for SP to retain that part of the route. This 2008 photograph was taken at USG's open pit quarry in the Fish Creek Mountains where gypsum is still mined, then transported via a 26-mile narrow gauge (three feet) private railway for processing at the Plaster City plant. (Deutsch.)

The ICC approved SP's $18.1 million sale to San Diego, or rather to its newly formed Metropolitan Transit Development Board (MTDB). MTDB wanted the right-of-way for a trolley system. SD&AE's transfer was considered part sale and part donation. SP estimated that the total value of the railroad was at least $80 million. This 1964 photograph shows the Plaster City station where MTDB's right-of-way ended. (PSRMA-ES.)

Six

TROLLEYS, FREIGHT, AND TOURISTS
A NEW ERA

Hurricane Kathleen wiped out the line in 1976. The San Diego Metropolitan Transit Development Board bought it from Southern Pacific in 1979 for an interurban transit system after stipulating that SP restore it to operating condition. Pragmatically, the future of Spreckels's railroad was quite uncertain.

SP wanted to retain profitable routes. Accordingly, it kept the 18-mile section between Plaster City and El Centro. It was minimally hurt by the storm, relatively easy to maintain and operate, and reliably profitable. SP also desired to keep the stretch between San Diego and San Ysidro, but MTDB would not agree to the sale without that westernmost piece, so it was included. Mexico owned 44 miles of track, not included in the sale, but did not possess even a single locomotive or railcar of its own. The railroad was now chopped up and under control of multiple owners. The traditional life of the SD&A(E) Railway appeared to be over.

The Interstate Commerce Commission required that freight service be maintained. MTDB, only interested in running light rail, sought to contract with a freight carrier. Notably, automobiles and trucks were positioned as primary movers of both passengers and cargo at that time. Floods, fires, earthquakes, environmental concerns, border security issues, vandalism, and expensive rehabilitation of infrastructure would be inevitable, regardless of who ran the railroad. What will become of this jinxed anachronism?

This chapter briefly summarizes diverse entities associated with the metamorphosis of the railroad to its new identity. Among them may be individuals or groups that possess the motivation, resourcefulness, energy, and tenacity of Spreckels himself. While the future of the *Impossible Railroad* is still uncertain, and more closures of the line should be expected, perhaps the passionate Spreckels spirit still lives in the current and future caretakers who will allow his *Impossible Railroad* to survive.

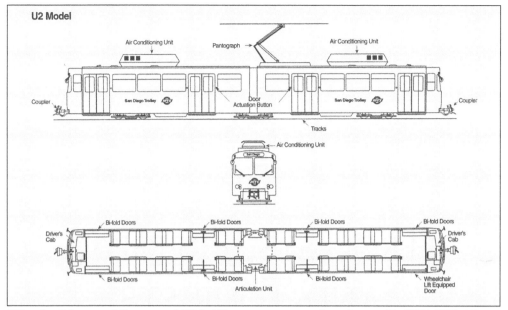

SP's sale of the now fully restored SD&AE was consummated on August 20, 1979. SD&AE was reorganized as a Nevada nonprofit corporation two months thereafter. The San Diego Trolley, Inc., was created by MTDB in August 1980 to operate and maintain the new transportation system. Initially, German-built Siemens-Duewag U2 light rail vehicles were utilized. This diagram illustrates the U2 vehicle configuration. (Scheuerman.)

Preparations for light rail began with rehabilitating part of SD&AE's right-of-way. On July 26, 1981, passenger service was unveiled between downtown San Diego (shown), now called Centre City by the transit company, and San Ysidro, just north of the Mexican border. It was built for $80 million using local funds. (Scheuerman.)

This scene, north of the Mexican border looking northward, displays a trolley headed toward San Ysidro, the end of the line. Double tracks serve that route. Tracks diverging toward the right of the picture continue south across the border and are on SD&AE's mainline. Some other trolley routes established since the early 1980s follow SD&AE's branch lines. (Scheuerman.)

In 2005, Metropolitan Transit System (MTS) replaced MTDB. Today, light rail serves three routes citywide. 37 million passengers ride annually on 53 miles of double track utilizing 134 cars and 53 stations. Only 57 percent of the $47-million annual operating costs are covered by fares. City sales tax, plus state and federal sources, subsidize the rest. (Deutsch.)

In 1979, a 10-year contract was executed by MTDB with the Willis Kyle Organization to continue freight operations as San Diego & Arizona Eastern Transportation Company. Kyle bought the six SP switching locomotives (EMD SW-8) remaining in San Diego. Four powerful GP9 road diesels, including No. 102 pictured here, were purchased elsewhere. Kyle arranged with Mexico to operate south of the border. (PSRMA.)

The *Impossible Railroad* was in service again, but not for long. In January 1980, heavy rains fell, resulting in washouts in the desert and Mexico. Floods in Tijuana were the worst on record. This image reflects storm damage in Imperial Valley. Repairs were promptly made by Kyle north of the border, but operations were delayed until tracks were repaired in Mexico. (Barnes.)

This Kyle caboose, tinted blue, sports the flying goose motif. All rolling stock in Kyle's inventory carried the same logo. When photographed in 1980, this railcar and the rest of its train were stranded at Dos Cabezas after tracks and bridges in both directions washed out. The crew was evacuated by helicopter. (Barnes.)

By January 1983, Mexico completed flood damage repairs and Kyle resumed operations. After 1976's Hurricane Kathleen, Interstate 8 drainage in Imperial Valley was rerouted to protect the freeway, causing SD&AE washouts whenever it rained. To minimize this, berms were crafted from material quarried from 200-foot-high Sugarloaf Mountain, the hill of non-marine Miocene conglomerate and sandstone behind Kyle's train in this photograph. (Barnes.)

1983 was a wet year. Winter and spring rains were comparatively gentle, causing no catastrophic flooding or damage. Unfortunately, as temperatures heated up toward summertime, lush green vegetation emerging after springtime showers dried out, producing tinder for a fire erupting in Carrizo Gorge. Lightning? Spark? Arson? Who knows? On June 18, 1983, two trestles east of Tunnel #6 burned down. These two views of distorted, gnarled tracks on one of the trestles display the impact of excessive heat on steel rails. The Desert Line ceased operations, this time, indefinitely! Alas, *Impossible Railroad's* curse still lingered. Kyle attempted to call it quits in October 1983, but its request for abandonment was denied. The ICC noted that SD&AE is obligated to provide common carrier rail service. Nevertheless, Kyle stopped operating shortly thereafter. (Barnes.)

MTDB contracted with Texas railcar leasing company RailTex, Inc., to provide freight operations as San Diego and Imperial Valley Railroad (SD&IV), RailTex's first railroad. On October 15, 1984, SD&IV began operating from San Diego to El Cajon along an SD&AE branch line, and from San Diego to San Ysidro on the mainline. Because it shared tracks with trolleys, it was restricted to nighttime operations. The San Ysidro engine house is shown above. On August 1, 1986, SD&IV contracted with Mexico to haul freight. Below, No. 5911 waits adjacent to Tijuana's station for reentry to the United States. Commodities transported included propane, metal, malt, barley, and lumber. SD&IV's operations proved profitable, exchanging cargo with Atchison, Topeka, and Santa Fe Railway (later, BNSF Railway) from the north. (Scheuerman.)

Carrizo Gorge remained impassable since the 1983 trestle-destroying fire. In 1986, a fire burned Tunnel #16 in the Gorge for three days, causing both ends to collapse. This 2000 image shows a remnant of the block signal and what used to be the west portal. Evidently, nature claimed the deserted roadbed over time. (Deutsch.)

In 1988, Carrizo Gorge's Tunnel #8 caught fire and partially collapsed. Multiple faults and nearby springs led to problematic groundwater seepage, flooding the east end. In 1989, SD&IV began repairing the Desert Line, replacing the two burned trestles and beginning repairs to Tunnel #8. Here, new metal supports are visible on the western end of #8's charred interior. Unfortunately, insurance money ran out before repairs were completed. (PSRMA.)

Opening Carrizo Gorge was beyond SD&IV's reach, yet it remained the only operator ever to achieve steady profits for the *Impossible Railroad*. It renewed its 10-year contract with MTDB in 1994 and 2004, sometimes moving over 6,500 cars annually. Since trains no longer operated through the Gorge, it became what law enforcement calls "an attractive nuisance." Hikers, cyclists, and even trans-border migrants evading border checkpoint screening took advantage of the railroad's level roadbed and gentle grade. The famous Goat Canyon trestle, unreachable by most, drew hardy nature-lovers and adventure-seekers, like the backpackers at Tunnel #20 above. Access to the railroad right-of-way was, and is, strictly illegal. Trespass restrictions were initiated, including locked tunnel gates, shown on the right, ticket-issuing railroad police patrols, and other security measures. (Deutsch above, PSRMA right.)

In February 2000, RailAmerica acquired RailTex and, hence, SD&IV. Years earlier, on July 4, 1997, a group of construction workers, railroad museum members, and businessmen formed Carrizo Gorge Railway, Inc. (CZRY) to open up Carrizo Gorge, obtain freight rights, and potentially run excursions along the SD&AE, including south of the border. In 2001, a new subsidiary of CZRY, Ferrocarriles Peninsulares del Noroeste, S.A. de C.V., was awarded a 25-year contract to operate the Mexican portion of the line, replacing SD&IV as freight carrier. Shortly thereafter, CZRY ran its first freight service between Tijuana and Tecate. SD&IV had no interest in or funds for repairing collapsed tunnels and bridges. Terms to carry freight on the Desert Line between Division and Plaster City were negotiated between the two companies and, on March 1, 2002, approved by owner MTDB. SD&IV retained freight rights between San Diego and San Ysidro (15 miles) and on the El Cajon branch line (18 miles) and still operates on those routes. CZRY's leased "Spirit" locomotives are shown here, proudly crossing Interstate 8 in Ocotillo in 2005. (Kahan.)

CZRY began restoration of the Desert Line in 2002 after obtaining private investment funds. The list of tunnels NOT requiring repair seemed shorter than the list needing to be fixed. CZRY "daylighted" Mexico's Tunnel #3 that caught fire and collapsed in April 1999. Its west portal, made of concrete, was preserved and is shown here in the background. Tunnel #3½, sheltering these gentlemen, reverted to its original designation, #3. CRZY also restored Tunnels #2 and #4 after fires broke out there. (PSRMA.)

Opening tunnels required monumental manpower and money. Collapsed Tunnel #8 was cleared the summer of 2003, now lined with concrete. CZRY's epic progress with #16 on January 13, 2004, is captured here. Three excavators and loaders working in tandem as a bucket brigade are devouring material blocking the eastern tunnel entrance. Despite recurring landslides, Tunnel #16 was opened in February 2004. (Kahan.)

After 20 years and $10 million, SD&AE's Carrizo Gorge was finally open! In May 2004, CZRY initiated trains from Imperial Valley to San Diego, primarily carrying sand for construction. It was a win-win situation for CZRY. Drifting sand (shown) was problematic, needing to be cleared from tracks anyway. December 30, 2004, was the first revenue freight service to Plaster City's interchange with the Union Pacific Railroad. (Union Pacific bought SP in 1996.) (Kahan.)

Was Spreckels reincarnated in CZRY? Against all odds, CZRY repaired, replaced, restored, or rehabilitated tracks, ties, timbers, tunnels, and trestles after damage from fires, natural elements, vandals, and prolonged neglect. Were tunnels too low to accommodate modern double-stack containers? No problem! CZRY just lowered the floors, evidenced by this impressive trestle-crossing in November 2005! Grain, scrap metal, barley, and lumber were rolling again. (Kahan.)

Challenges persisted, as this June 2004 derailment suggests. On October 17, 2008, the Desert Line was closed indefinitely for $8 million of safety and reliability upgrades. CZRY, now under new management, continues freight operations in Mexico after interchanging with SD&IV in San Ysidro. Transporting passengers requires higher standards of safety and prohibitively high insurance costs. Accordingly, resumption of passenger service through Carrizo Gorge is unlikely in the near future. (Kahan.)

San Diego County Railway Museum, renamed Pacific Southwest Railway Museum Association (PSRMA) and known as San Diego Railroad Museum during 1988–2000, was formed in 1961. The nonprofit volunteer organization preserves history, traditions, and experience of railroading through its Campo Railroad Museum, La Mesa Depot Museum, and Southwest Railway Library. PSRMA's 1916-built Campo Depot, seen here 90 years later, is along the SD&AE right-of-way. (Deutsch.)

PSRMA acquired rolling stock and a can-do attitude. Volunteers restore and maintain equipment, facilities, and tracks. By agreement with MTS, excursions operate from the Campo depot on SD&AE's tracks during weekends, holidays, and special events. Posing here on January 4, 1986, is the first crew running the first public train on the first day of its 16-mile (26-kilometer) round-trip Golden State Limited to Miller Creek. (Helm.)

Since 1986, PSRMA has offered public and charter rail excursions to backcountry destinations using restored vintage equipment. Its Campo and La Mesa depots contain displays and exhibits. PSRMA intermittently provides locations and equipment for movie, television, and commercial filming. In this picture are some of the 500 passengers participating in the first museum trip to Jacumba on April 29, 1989. (Scheuerman.)

Briefly before Carrizo Gorge was opened up, PSRMA and CZRY collaborated to conduct excursions by rail into the Gorge. In 1999, Motorcar Operators West, a group of speeder-owners, was fortunate to experience the breathtaking views by rail as far as the blocked tunnels. This image shows them crossing Campo Creek Viaduct over highway 94 on the way to the Gorge. (Deutsch.)

PSRMA's volunteers, like the one toiling here in a steam locomotive's smokebox, continue to work individually, and sometimes side-by-side with CZRY, to keep SD&AE's route open. Its equipment, (wo)manpower, and ingenuity provide restoration, maintenance, excursions, and education in support of its mission to preserve and interpret regional railroading. The energy and determination of its member-volunteers would make John Spreckels proud that his "Impossible Railroad" will continue into the future. (PSRMA.)

BIBLIOGRAPHY

Adams, H. Austin. *The Man John D. Spreckels*. San Diego, CA: Press of Frye & Smith, 1924.

Anspach DS. Compendium, *Motorcar Operators West San Diego and Arizona Eastern Excursion*, San Diego Railroad Museum. (October 23 and 24, 1999).

Copenhaver, George C. "Main Stem: Geology of the San Diego & Arizona Eastern Railway, San Diego and Imperial Counties, California, U.S.A. and Baja California, Mexico." *Geology and History of Southeastern San Diego County, California* (Geologic Field Trip Guidebook for 2005 and 2006): 63–90.

Dodge, Richard V. "San Diego's 'Impossible Railroad.'" *Dispatcher* #6 (June 29, 1956), Railway Historical Society of San Diego, California, Pacific Southwest Railway Museum, Eric Sanders Collection: 1–6.

Friedman, Ralph. "No manana, muchado." *Trains* (June 1951).

Hanft, Robert M. *San Diego & Arizona: The Impossible Railroad*. Glendale, CA: Trans-Anglo Books, 1984.

http://en.wikipedia.org/wiki/John_D._Spreckels Accessed May 31, 2010.

McGrew, Clarence Alan. *City of San Diego and San Diego County: The Birthplace of California*. Chicago, IL: The American Historical Society, 1922.

O'Herin, Charles M. *Prototypes for Modelers: Volume 1, San Diego & Arizona Railway*. Tacoma, WA: Link Pen Publishing, 2006.

Pourade R. F. *The History of San Diego, Gold in the Sun*. San Diego, CA: Union-Tribune Publishing Company, 1965.

Richter D. S. "All-time Steam Roster SD&A–SD&AE." *Pacific News* (Number 104, June 1970):4–8.

San Diego biographies John D. Spreckels (1853–1926). sandiegohistory.org/bio/spreckels/spreckels.htm Accessed May 31, 2010.

Scheuerman Geoffrey T. and R. Lamar. *San Diego & Arizona Rwy.: The New Millennium*. Unpublished manuscript. 2010.

"The War that Ended in a Railroad Caboose!" *Southern Pacific Bulletin* (June 1957), sdrm.org/history/sda/spbulletin/1957.html Accessed May 31, 2010: 14–16.

Wilson, John A. "Formidable Places: Building a Railroad in the Carriso Gorge." *Journal of San Diego History* (Volume 40, Number 4, Fall 1994): 178–197.

PACIFIC SOUTHWEST RAILWAY MUSEUM ASSOCIATION

THE PACIFIC SOUTHWEST RAILWAY MUSEUM (PSRMA), established in 1961, is an all-volunteer 501(c)3 non-profit educational organization dedicated to the preservation and interpretation of railroads in the Pacific Southwest. The Museum consists of three components:

CAMPO RAILROAD MUSEUM
The Campo museum is an 8½-acre living history interpretive center located in the rural backcountry town of Campo, California, 50 miles east of San Diego. It maintains an onsite collection of over eighty pieces of rail equipment. Excursions on vintage trains, exhibits, and tours are available on weekends.

LA MESA DEPOT MUSEUM
La Mesa Depot is in the heart of La Mesa, California, ten miles east of San Diego. The completely restored depot, built in 1894, contains exhibits and displays a freight train outside.

SOUTHWEST RAILWAY LIBRARY
The PSRMA library, located at Campo, contains one of the most extensive collections of railroad maps, books, documents, ephemera, and photographs in the West. Researchers and interested parties may access collections by appointment.

Please explore and experience the wonderful world of southwest railroading. Memberships are available. For complete information, including train ride schedules, visit
www.psrm.org

La Mesa Depot and PSRMA Business Office
4695 Nebo Drive
La Mesa, CA 91941-5259
(619) 465-7776 / (619) 465-PSRM (recorded message)

Campo Depot (Main Facility and Train Rides)
State Highway 94 & Forrest Gate Road
Campo, California
(619) 478-9937 weekends

Visit us at
arcadiapublishing.com

CPSIA information can be obtained
at www.ICGtesting.com
Printed in the USA
LVHW061602191121
703839LV00003B/610